Free Money for People in the Arts

ALSO BY LAURIE BLUM

Free Money for Humanities Students

Free Money for Science Students

Free Money for Professional Studies

Free Money for Humanities and Social Sciences

Free Money for Mathematics and Natural Sciences

Free Money for Professional Studies

Free Money for Undergraduate Study

Free Money for Graduate Study

Free Money for Foreign Study

Free Money for Small Businesses and Entrepreneurs

How to Invest in Real Estate Using Free Money

Free Money for People in the Arts

Laurie Blum

Collier Books
Macmillan Publishing Company
New York
Maxwell Macmillan Canada
Toronto
Maxwell Macmillan International
New York   Oxford   Singapore   Sydney

Collier Books
Macmillan Publishing Company
866 Third Avenue
New York, NY 10022

Maxwell Macmillan Canada, Inc.
1200 Eglinton Avenue East, Suite 200
Don Mills, Ontario M3C 3N1

Macmillan Publishing Company is part of the
Maxwell Communication Group of Companies.

Library of Congress Cataloging-in-Publication Data

Blum, Laurie.
　　Free money for people in the arts / Laurie Blum.
　　　　p.　cm.
　　Includes bibliographical references and index.
　　ISBN 0-02-028175-7
　　1. Arts—Scholarships, fellowships, etc.—United States—
Directories.　I. Title.
NX398.B58　1991
700'.79'73—dc20　　　　　　　　90-22911

Macmillan books are available at special discounts for bulk purchases for sales promotions, premiums, fund-raising, or educational use. For details, contact:

　　Special Sales Director
　　Macmillan Publishing Company
　　866 Third Avenue
　　New York, NY 10022

10 9 8 7 6 5 4 3 2 1
Designed by Nancy Sugihara
Printed in the United States of America

Contents

I

---

*Direct Grants
to Individuals,
by Subject*

Introduction

This is a book I have wanted to write for a long time. Although I have written several books on grant monies available for various purposes—undergraduate education, graduate school, small business development, and real estate development—I have always felt that the most needed book in the Free Money series was one for people who have chosen that most difficult of professions, creative art. I use the word *artist* in the broadest sense to encompass a range of disciplines such as dance, film, theater, writing, and the visual arts. These are precarious times for the arts. Federal funding is diminishing and may be on the verge of extinction. The creative artist has special needs: he or she needs time to think, to try out various styles, and to grow. Few have the luxury of financial support to facilitate this process. This book offers a wide range of potential sources of financial support to help artists in their chosen careers.

How to Use This Book

The funding sources listed in this book are divided into four categories. Part I lists sources of funding available to individuals by subject. Subject listings are divided into broad categories such as dance, theater, and visual arts, which in turn are broken down into more specific topics; for instance, under theater

3

you'll find acting, multimedia, performance art, and playwriting.

Part II lists sources of funding (again, to individuals) that are geographically restricted, usually to residents of a state or region. These listings are organized alphabetically by state.

Part III lists fiscal sponsorship monies—grants that are awarded to an individual who is sponsored by a nonprofit, tax-exempt organization. A brief introduction (page 205) explains how the sponsorship works.

Part IV lists federal agencies that give money to artists, and is organized by subject area within each agency listing.

Following these listings of sources are sample proposals to give you an idea of what goes into a typical arts funding proposal.

How to Apply for Funding

Go through this book and mark off all the listings that may give you money. Pay close attention to the restrictions and eliminate the least likely foundations. Although few of the foundations in this book require an application fee, the effort you'll have to put in will probably limit you to five applications. Write or call the most likely foundations to get a copy of their guidelines (where no contact is listed, begin your letter "To Whom It May Concern"). If you call, just request the guidelines—please don't interrogate the poor person who answers the phone.

Grant applications take time to fill out. You will have to provide personal information about yourself. Often you will be required to write a statement of artistic purpose. Slides, musical tapes, videotapes of performance pieces, or samples of your writing will often be requested, as will academic and occupational background information. You may be asked to include personal references; call each person you plan to list to ask if he or she feels comfortable giving you a reference. As obvious as this sounds, be neat! You may very well prepare a top-notch proposal, but it won't be received well if it's done in a sloppy manner. Proposals should always be typed and double spaced. Be sure to make a copy of the proposal for your records. I've learned the hard way that there is nothing worse than having to reconstruct your proposal when you didn't keep a copy and the foundation can't find the original you sent. You may be asked for your tax return and other financial records (don't worry, you won't be penalized for having money in the bank or being a successful artist; quite the contrary, it usually works in your favor). Remember, you have to sell yourself and persuade the grantors to give money to you and not to someone else.

Be sure to read the sample grant proposals at the end of the book. They are actual examples of typical arts proposals, and I'm happy to say they received excellent funding.

One Final Note

By the time this book is published, some of the information contained here will have changed. Most of it will not have. Because names, amounts, deadlines, and so on are constantly changing, it's wise to double check all information when the time comes to send in your proposal.

Good luck.

Architecture

American Academy and Institute of Arts and Letters
633 West 155th Street
New York, NY 10032
(212) 368–5900

Program/Award: Arnold W. Brunner Memorial Prize in Architecture
Description: Prize to an architect who contributes to architecture as an art.
Restrictions: N/A
Type of art: Architecture
$ given: $1,000 per award
Number of awards: 1 award annually
Contact: Lydia Kaim, Assistant to Executive Director
Application information: No applications accepted. By nomination from membership only. Recipient is chosen by a committee of architects drawn from the membership and appointed by the Board.

American Academy in Rome
41 East 65th Street
New York, NY 10021-6508
(212) 517–4200

Program/Award: Rome Prize Fellowships
Description: Fellowships for independent work. Provided in cooperation with the NEA, NEH, and other foundations. Supported projects must be conducted at the American Academy in Rome facilities.
Restrictions: U.S. citizenship. No age limit. Applicants must be

licensed professionals (if license is required in the field) with at least 7 years of work experience in the field. Preference given to artists and scholars of outstanding promise or achievement.

Type of art: Architecture, Landscape Architecture, Design, Musical Composition, Creative Writing, Painting, Sculpture, and various humanistic scholarly studies

$ given: $6,200 annual stipend plus housing, studio space, and travel allowance. Fellows with children receive additional $1,980 applicable to housing costs for accommodations outside the Academy. Maximum total funding for 2-year fellowship, approx. $17,800.

Number of grants: 24–30 per year. Most fellowships for 1-year period (September through August). Some for 2 years; 6-month fellowships in design arts also available.

Contact: N/A

Application information: Write for official application materials, specifying particular field of interest.

Deadline: November 15

Note: Fellows are strongly urged to begin study of Italian before leaving for Rome.

American Institute of Architects
1735 New York Avenue, NW
Washington, DC 20006
(202) 626–7300

Program/Award: R. S. Reynolds Memorial Award

Description: Design award given for a permanent significant work of architecture in the creation of which aluminum has been an important contributing factor.

Restrictions: N/A

Type of art: Architecture

$ given: $25,000 per award

Number of awards: 1 annually

Application information: Write for nomination form and deadline information.

Graham Foundation for Advanced Study in the Fine Arts
Four West Burton Place
Chicago, IL 60610
(312) 787–4071

Description: Grants to individuals and institutions for projects relating to contemporary architecture, planning, and the study of urban design problems. Preference given to younger creative architects.

Restrictions: No funding given for projects undertaken in pursuit of a degree.

Type of art: Architecture

$ given: Up to $10,000 per grant. Total of $662,721 awarded in 1989.

Number of grants: 87 grants given in 1989

Contact: The Director

Application information: Letter of application should include project description, statement of value and purposes to be served, budget, and qualifications of those undertaking the work.

Deadlines: June 1 and December 1

National Institute for Architectural Education
30 West 22nd Street
New York, NY 10010
(212) 924–7000

Program/Award: William Van Alen Architect Memorial Fellowships; Sidney L. Katz Memorial Prizes

Description: Fellowships, awarded competitively, for travel and/or study abroad. Winners are required to report periodically on their experiences graphically and in writing.

Restrictions: Participants in the competition must be students enrolled in architectural or engineering school (or equivalent), full or part-time, working toward a professional degree. The school may incorporate this competition into the curriculum, but must hold preliminary judgment to select best projects. Entries are accepted from outside the U.S. for this international competition.

Type of art: Architecture
$ given: $6,000 per First Prize (2); $2,500 per Second Prize (2); $1,500 per Third Prize (2); $750 per First Honorable Mention (2); $200 per Honorable Mention (6). Two Katz Prizes of $250 each are awarded for outstanding presentation.
Number of awards: 16 per competition
Contact: "William Van Alen Fellowships"
Application information: Write for official application form.

National Institute for Architectural Education
30 West 22nd Street
New York, NY 10010
(212) 924–7000

Program/Award: Lloyd Warren Fellowship/Paris Prize; Arnold A. Arbeit Memorial Prizes
Description: Fellowships, awarded competitively, for travel and/or study abroad. Winners are required to report periodically on their experiences graphically and in writing.
Restrictions: Participants in the competition must have or anticipate receiving their first professional degree in architecture from a U.S. school by December of the year of competition. The school may incorporate this competition into its curriculum, but must hold preliminary judgment to select best projects.
Type of art: Architecture
$ given: $8,000 First Prize for minimum 3-month period; $6,000 Second Prize for minimum 2-month period; $2,000 Third Prize for minimum 1-month period; $1,000 per Honorable Mention (5 awarded). Two Arbeit Prizes of $200 each are awarded for outstanding presentation.
Number of awards: 10 annually
Contact: "Lloyd Warren Fellowship"
Application information: Write for official application form.
Deadline: May 10 for Warren Fellowship; March 1 for Paris and Arbeit prizes

Rotch Traveling Scholarship in Architecture
c/o Shepley, Bulfinch, Richardson, and Abbott
40 Broad Street, 6th Floor
Boston, MA 02109
(617) 423–1700

Program/Award: Rotch Traveling Scholarship
Description: Scholarships for 8 months of foreign travel and study in the field of architecture.
Restrictions: Applicant must be a U.S. citizen, no older than 35, with a degree from an accredited school of architecture plus at least one year experience in an architectural firm in Massachusetts; or a degree from an accredited Massachusetts school of architecture plus one year experience in an architectural office not necessarily in Massachusetts. No Rotch Scholar may hold another traveling scholarship simultaneously or be employed during the period without specific permission.
Type of art: Architecture
$ given: $16,000 per award plus $1,500 upon completion of report
Number of awards: 1 annually
Contact: Hugh Shepley, Secretary
Application information: Write for official application forms.
Deadline: January

Washington University
School of Architecture
Box 1079
St. Louis, MO 63130
(314) 889–6200

Program/Award: James Harrison Steedman Memorial Fellowship in Architecture
Description: Award made on the basis of design competition. Fellowship for architectural graduates for a year of travel and study abroad.
Restrictions: Open to architects, regardless of age, up to 8 years after the receipt of their professional degrees from accredited schools.
Type of art: Architecture

$ given: $20,000 stipend per award
Number of awards: 1 biennially
Contact: Steedman Governing Committee
Application information: Applications should be made to the committee.
Deadline: December 15, biennially

Also see: Innovative Design Fund/DESIGN
　　　　　Institute of International Education Cintas/PRINT-MAKING
　　　　　National Endowment for the Arts/DESIGN

Design

American Society of Interior Designers Educational Foundation
1430 Broadway
New York, NY 10018
(212) 944–9220

Program/Award: Environmental Design Award
Description: Annual award presented to an individual, organization, institution, or project group in the U.S. or Canada to encourage the desirable interaction of the design professions in a holistic approach to the design process when solving environmental problems.
Restrictions: Open to individuals, organizations, institutions, and project groups in the U.S. and Canada.
Type of art: Design
$ given: $4,000 per award
Number of awards: 1 annually
Contact: Robert H. Angle, Executive Director
Application information: Write for application form. Entry submissions should stress an interdisciplinary approach to real environmental problems, emphasizing research as well as design ability in their problem-solving process. Jury members

will give special consideration to those projects where the award grant would serve as seed money for obtaining additional funding for the planning and design stage, thereby enhancing the possibility of project completion.

Deadline: February 15

National Endowment for the Arts
Design Arts Program, Room 625
1100 Pennsylvania Avenue, NW
Washington, DC 20506
(202) 682–5437

Program/Award: Design Arts Program

Description: Grants for design projects that have the potential for producing results of exceptional merit and national or regional significance. Categories: Design Advancement (theory, research, education); U.S.A. Fellowships (independent study for designers in mid-career); Distinguished Designer Fellowships (outstanding career contributions); Project Grants for Individuals; and grant programs for organizations and state agencies.

Restrictions: U.S. citizens or permanent residents only.

Type of art: Architecture, Landscape Architecture, Urban Design, Historical Preservation, Planning, Interior Design, Industrial Design, Graphic Design, Fashion Design

$ given: Up to $20,000 per U.S.A. Fellowship and Distinguished Designer Fellowship; up to $15,000 per Advancement Project Grants to Individuals

Number of awards: 148 in all categories in fiscal year 1988

Contact: Randolph McAusland, Director

Application information: Write for informational brochure.

Deadline: Varies

Also see: American Academy in Rome/ARCHITECTURE

Media Arts

Film

Academy of Motion Picture Arts and Sciences
Academy Foundation
8949 Wilshire Boulevard
Beverly Hills, CA 90211
(213) 278–8990

Program/Award: Student Film Awards
Description: Annual awards for student filmmaking.
Restrictions: Applicant must be enrolled in accredited college, university, or art school.
Type of art: Film
$ given: Three categories of awards: $1,000 Achievement, $750 Honorary, $500 Merit
Number of awards: Maximum of 13 annually
Contact: Richard Miller
Application information: Write for guidelines and application form.
Deadline: April 1

American Film and Video Association
920 Barnsdale Road
LaGrange Park, IL 60525
(312) 482–4000

Program/Award: John Grierson Award, American Film and Video Festival
Description: Cash award to film/video maker who shows outstanding talent in the social documentary field.
Restrictions: Applicant must be a finalist in the American Film and Video Festival. Work must be a social documentary (dramatizations, instructional films, and public relations films ineligible). Work must be first production of the director.
Type of art: Film, Video
$ given: $500 per award

Number of awards: 1 annually
Contact: Ron MacIntyre, AFVA Executive Director
Application information: Official entry blank plus detailed professional biography required.
Deadline: January 2 for Festival; notification in May

American Film Institute
2021 North Western Avenue
P.O. Box 27999
Los Angeles, CA 90027
(213) 856–7640

Program/Award: The Academy Internship Program
Description: Opportunity for a limited number of promising new directors to learn by observing established directors at work during the making of a feature or TV film.
Restrictions: Applicant must be at least 21 years old, be a U.S. citizen or permanent resident, and have directed several short films. Must be available to interview at own expense.
Type of art: Film
$ given: Maximum of $5,000: stipend of $150 per week of internship in town, $200 per week on location
Number of awards: 5 for 1989–90
Contact: Teresa Martin, Director, Distribution and Production Programs
Application information: Applicants are required to submit a 2-page application form and résumé, and may be asked to submit a film or videotape they directed.
Deadline: June 30

American Film Institute
2021 North Western Avenue
P.O. Box 27999
Los Angeles, CA 90027
(213) 856–7722

Program/Award: Directing Workshop for Women

Description: Workshop memberships and budgets to make videotapes to help film industry women develop their skills in feature and TV directing. Biennial awards of 18 months' duration.

Restrictions: Applicants must be professional women who have considerable experience in feature and TV films, but who have not yet had the opportunity to direct.

Type of art: Film

$ given: $5,000 cash budget per award

Number of awards: 15 for 1989–90

Contact: Teresa Martin, Director, Distribution and Production Programs

Application information: Applicants are requested to submit a résumé or brief biography of professional background in addition to the application form.

Deadline: Varies

American Film Institute
2021 North Western Avenue
P.O. Box 27999
Los Angeles, CA 90027
(213) 856–7696

Program/Award: Independent Filmmaker Program

Description: Grants to support the film and video projects of independent filmmakers. (The Institute also awards a number of advanced production grants to experienced film and video artists for complete or supplemental funding of proposed work in narrative, animation, experimental, and/or documentary video and filmmaking.)

Restrictions: Applicants must be U.S. citizens or permanent residents not enrolled as students in an institution of higher learning at any time within 3 months prior to application or during the life of the grant.

Type of art: Film, Video

$ given: $500 to $20,000 per grant

Number of awards: Approx. 14 per year

Contact: Karin Kary, coordinator, Independent Filmmaker Program
Application information: Write for application forms after July 1. Applicants must submit a film or videotape for which they had directorial responsibility—broadcast-quality videotape and 16mm or 35mm film only. Selection is made on the basis of the applicant's creativity and technical competence.
Deadline: September 15

Arts Extension Service, Division of Continuing Education
Goodell Building
University of Massachusetts
Amherst, MA 01003
(413) 545-2360

Program/Award: New England Film Festival
Description: Cash awards for regional competition.
Restrictions: Limited to residents of Connecticut, Massachusetts, Maine, New Hampshire, Rhode Island, and Vermont; or to students who completed their films while enrolled at colleges in these states.
Type of art: Film
$ given: $1,000 *Boston Globe* Best of Festival; 4 awards totaling $2,000 to students and independents; Honorable Mentions
Number of awards: N/A
Contact: N/A
Application information: Write for guidelines and application forms.

Boston Film and Video Foundation
1126 Boylston
Boston, MA 02215
(617) 536-1540

Program/Award: New England Film/Video Fellowship Program
Description: Grants for completion of works-in-progress and new works, also for use of facilities and equipment.

Restrictions: Limited to residents of Connecticut, Massachusetts, Maine, New Hampshire, Rhode Island, and Vermont. Applicants must be U.S. citizens, over age 18. Full-time students and projects associated with degree programs are not eligible. Organizations and collaborative groups may not apply. Noncommercial projects only.

Type of art: Film, Video

$ given: $5,000 for completion of works-in-progress or new works; up to $5,000 for facility and equipment use

Number of awards: N/A

Contact: N/A

Application information: Write for guidelines and application form.

Pittsburgh Filmmakers
The Media Arts Center
205 Oakdale Avenue
P.O. Box 7467
Pittsburgh, PA 15213
(412) 681–5449

Program/Award: Mid-Atlantic Regional Arts Fellowship Program

Description: Grants to regional media artists.

Restrictions: Applicants must have been residents of Delaware, Maryland, District of Columbia, New Jersey, Pennsylvania, or West Virginia for at least one year prior to application. Individuals only; organizations may not apply. Full-time students not eligible.

Type of art: Media Art, Film, Video

$ given: Maximum of $5,000 per grant. Pennsylvania residents may request up to $7,000 per grant.

Number of grants: N/A

Contact: Matthew Yokobosky, Fellowship Coordinator

Application information: Write or call for guidelines and application form.

Rocky Mountain Film Center
Hunter 102
P.O. Box 316
University of Colorado
Boulder, CO 80309–0316
(303) 492–1531

Program/Award: Western States Media Fellowship Program
Description: Annual regional grant program for media artists.
Restrictions: Applicants must have been residents of Alaska, Arizona, California, Colorado, Hawaii, Idaho, Montana, Nevada, New Mexico, Oregon, Utah, Washington, Wyoming, or the Pacific Territories for at least one year prior to application. Individuals only; organizations may not apply. Full-time students not eligible.
Type of art: Media Art, Film, Video; no funding for script development
$ given: $1,000 to $5,000 per grant; the Washington State Arts Commission also awards $5,000 to the highest ranked recipient from Washington.
Number of awards: N/A
Contact: Patti Bruck, Program Coordinator
Application information: Write or call for guidelines and application forms.

The San Francisco Foundation
685 Market Street
Suite 910
San Francisco, CA 94105
(415) 543–0223

Program/Award: James D. Phelan Awards in Art
Description: Awards to young California artists in various fields of art. Three awards each offered in printmaking and photography one year, in film and video the next year.
Restrictions: Native-born Californians only.
Type of art: Film, Video, Printmaking, Photography
$ given: $2,500 per award

Number of awards: 6 per year
Contact: N/A
Application information: Write to request details and annual
   deadlines.

Also see: American Film Institute, TV Workshop/OTHER
      MEDIA ART
      Anthology Film Archives Film Art Fund, Inc./VIDEO
      Appalshop/VIDEO
      Center for New Television/VIDEO
      Foundation for Independent Video and Film/VIDEO
      Image Film, Video Center/VIDEO
      Media Alliance/OTHER MEDIA ART

Video

Anthology Film Archives Film Art Fund, Inc.
32-34 Second Avenue
New York, NY 10003
(212) 505–5181

Program/Award: Jay Leyda Book Prize
Description: Project grants for film and video artists.
Restrictions: Applicant must be an individual writing on inde-
   pendent film or video.
Type of art: Film, Video
$ given: $2,000 per grant
Number of awards: 1
Contact: Sheila Divola, Administrative Director
Application information: Write for details.

Appalshop
P.O. Box 743
Whitesburg, KY 41858
(606) 633–0108

Program/Award: Southeast Media Fellowships
Description: Regional fellowships for media artists.
Restrictions: Limited to residents of Alabama, Florida, Georgia,

Kentucky, Louisiana, Mississippi, North Carolina, South Carolina, Tennessee, and Virginia.
Type of art: Film, Video, Media Art
$ given: $5,000 per fellowship
Number of awards: Up to 15 annually
Contact: N/A
Application information: Write for guidelines and application forms.

Checkerboard Foundation, Inc.
P.O. Box 222, Ansonia Station
New York, NY 10023

Program/Award: Checkerboard Foundation Video Awards
Description: Cash awards for video projects.
Restrictions: Limited to residents of New York who have previously completed a video project.
Type of art: Video
$ given: $5,000 to $10,000 per award
Number of awards: 2–4 per year
Contact: N/A
Application information: Write for guidelines and application.

Foundation for Independent Video and Film, Inc.
625 Broadway, 9th Floor
New York, NY 10012
(212) 473–3400

Program/Award: Donor–Advised Film Fund
Description: Funding for various grants and awards: Marjorie Benton Peace Film Award for completed film or video that best promotes understanding of peace issues; postproduction grant for work in progress that is substantially completed; and Beldon Fund Grants for production, editing, completion, or distribution of works dealing with environmental issues.
Restrictions: Applicant must be affiliated with a nonprofit organization. Institutional projects for internal or promotional use not eligible. Productions of public television stations not eligible. Student projects not eligible.

Type of art: Film, Video
$ given: $5,000 for Marjorie Benton Peace Film Award; $10,000 for postproduction grant; total of $20,000 annually for Beldon Fund Grants
Number of awards: At least 3 annually
Contact: N/A
Application information: Write for guidelines and application form.
Deadline: N/A

Image Film/Video Center
75 Bennett Street, Suite J-2
Atlanta, GA 30309
(404) 352–4225

Description: Competition in 5 categories of film and video: animation, narrative, documentary, student, and experimental.
Restrictions: Independently produced films only, in any form except 35mm. No limit to number of entries, but each must be submitted separately.
Type of art: Film, Video
$ given: $100 to $500 per award
Number of awards: 10 annually, 1 in each category
Contact: N/A
Application information: Write or call for guidelines.

Barbara Aronofsky Latham Memorial Grants
School of the Art Institute of Chicago
Columbus Drive at Jackson Boulevard
Chicago, IL 60603
(312) 443–3700

Program/Award: Video and Electronic Visualization Art
Description: Award for works-in-progress or new works of any form of experimental video or electronic visualization art, broadly interpreted.
Restrictions: Applicant must be at least 18 years old.
Type of art: Video, Media Art
$ given: $300 to $1,500 per grant

Number of awards: N/A
Contact: N/A
Application information: Write for guidelines and application forms.
Deadline: April 15

Niagara Council on the Arts
P.O. Box 937, Falls Station
Niagara Falls, NY 14303
(713) 278–8147

Program/Award: Video Production Grants
Description: Grants for video projects that relate to Niagara County. Special consideration is given to projects that make use of unique opportunities through access to cable television.
Restrictions: Projects must relate to Niagara County.
Type of art: Video
$ given: 3 grants of $3,000 each; 1 grant of $1,000
Number of awards: 4 grants annually
Contact: N/A
Application information: Write or call for guidelines and application form.

Also see: American Film and Video Association/FILM
American Film Institute, Independent Filmmaker Project/FILM
American Film Institute, TV Workshop/OTHER MEDIA ART
Boston Film and Video Foundation/FILM
Media Alliance/OTHER MEDIA ART
National Endowment for the Arts, Visual Arts/VISUAL ARTS–GENERAL
Pittsburgh Filmmakers/FILM
Rocky Mountain Film Center/FILM
The San Francisco Foundation/FILM

Other Media Art

American Film Institute
2021 North Western Avenue
P.O. Box 27999
Los Angeles, CA 90027
(213) 856–7743

Program/Award: TV Workshop/Artist Residencies
Description: Grants to artists for various media projects, including music videos and documentaries.
Restrictions: Applicants must be U.S. citizens.
Type of art: Video, Audio, Music
$ given: Varies according to project needs
Number of awards: N/A
Contact: Vicki Costello
Application information: Write or call for guidelines and application forms.

Media Alliance
c/o WNET
356 West 58th Street
New York, NY 10019
(212) 560–2919

Program/Award: On Line
Description: Discounts at participating commercial video and audio facilities.
Restrictions: N/A
Type of art: Media Art, Video, Audio
$ given: Varies according to needs of grant recipient's project and the participating video and audio facility
Number of awards: N/A
Contact: Lisa Overton, Program Director
Application information: Write for details.
Deadline: None; ongoing program

Also see: Appalshop/VIDEO
           Barbara Aronofsky Latham Memorial Grants/VIDEO

Pittsburgh Filmmakers/FILM
Rocky Mountain Film Center/FILM

Dance

Affiliate Artists Inc.
37 West 65th Street
New York, NY 10023
(212) 580–2000

Program/Award: Community Residences for Solo Performing
Artists
Description: Residency program of 1–6 weeks for various per-
forming artists.
Restrictions: Applicant must be U.S. citizen or permanent
resident with 3–10 years of professional performing experi-
ence.
Type of art: Dance, Music Performance (instrumental and vocal),
Theater
$ given: $1,000 stipend per week plus expenses
Number of awards: N/A
Contact: Carol Wolff, Director, Artist Recruitment and Qualifi-
cation
Application information: Write for application; specify disci-
pline.
Deadline: August 1

American Ballet Competition
P.O. Box 328
Philadelphia, PA 19105

Program/Award: American Ballet Competition
Description: ABC sponsors the American team at international
ballet competitions.
Restrictions: Vary according to competition.
Type of art: Dance

$ given: Maximum of $10,000 in stipends, which can be used for travel, accommodations, costumes, shoes, partners, coaches, music, and/or accompanist
Number of awards: Dependent upon international competition schedules.
Contact: N/A
Application information: Write for details.

Boston Ballet
553 Tremont Street
Boston, MA 02116
(617) 964–4070

Program/Award: Boston International Choreography Competition
Description: Competition of premiere works.
Restrictions: Work must not have been previously performed; not to exceed 10 minutes.
Type of art: Choreography
$ given: Awards of $3,000, $2,000, and $1,000
Number of awards: 3 per competition
Contact: N/A
Application information: Write for guidelines and application forms.

National Endowment for the Arts
Dance Program
Nancy Hanks Center
1100 Pennsylvania Avenue, NW
Washington, DC 20506
(202) 682–5435

Program/Award: Choreographers' Fellowships
Description: Grants to provide professional choreographers with financial assistance to promote artistic growth. These are not commissions. Work done during the fellowship period need not culminate in a performance. Fellowship funds may be

used for any project or activity that will aid a choreographer's creative development, including travel for dance-related purposes.

Restrictions: Only individual choreographers are eligible. Choreographers who are artistic directors of professional companies funded by the NEA Dance Program may not apply.

Type of art: Choreography

$ given: Fellowships awarded at levels of $7,500, $10,000, and $15,000

Number of awards: 85 for fiscal year 1989

Contact: Dance Program

Application information: Request guidelines for application procedures. Applicants should not specify level of funding requested; NEA panel will determine. Applicants should request 1-year fellowship period, but panel may recommend a limited number of 3-year fellowships.

Deadline: Early December; notification the following October

National Endowment for the Arts
Dance Program
Nancy Hanks Center
1100 Pennsylvania Avenue, NW
Washington, DC 20506
(202) 682–5435

Program/Award: Dance/Film/Video

Description: Assistance to organizations and individuals who use film or video to creatively preserve, enhance, and expand the art of dance. Grants are awarded primarily for projects in which dance takes precedence over the film or video art form.

Restrictions: Individuals or tax-exempt organizations in continuous operation for at least 3 years, with a professional managerial staff, the highest level of dancers, and proven fundraising ability. Grants are generally available only for projects involving filmmakers/videomakers who have had prior experience working with dance.

Type of art: Dance
$ given: Up to $15,000 per individual (most grants substantially less); $5,000 to $20,000 per organization
Number of awards: Total of 15 awards to individuals and organizations in fiscal year 1989
Contact: Dance Program
Application information: Write for guidelines and application procedures.
Deadline: Mid-November: notification following October

Also see: National Federation of Music Clubs/COMPOSITION

Music

Composition

Accademia Musicale Chigiana
Via di Citta, 89
53100 Siena, Italy
0039–577–46152

Program/Award: Alfredo Casella International Composition Contest
Description: Annual international composition contest.
Restrictions: Specific composition requirements may vary from year to year. Open to composers of any nationality and age. Compositions must be unpublished and not previously performed.
Type of art: Composition
$ given: 5,000,000 lire First Prize; 3,000,000 lire Second Prize may be awarded to other outstanding compositions
Number of awards: At least 1 annually
Contact: Concorso "Alfredo Casella," Accademia Musicale Chigiana
Application information: Compositions must be sent by registered mail or delivered, in quintuplicate, to: Accademia Musi-

cale Chigiana, Concorso "Alfredo Casella," at the address above. Further information available on request.
Deadline: October 1; notification by November 30

American Academy and Institute of Arts and Letters
633 West 155th Street
New York, NY 10032
(212) 368–5900

Program/Award: Marc Blitzstein Award for the Musical Theatre
Description: Award to a composer, lyricist, or librettist to encourage the creation of works of merit for the musical theater, given periodically.
Restrictions: N/A
Type of art: Composition
$ given: $2,500 per award
Number of awards: Periodic awards
Contact: Lydia Kaim, Assistant to Executive Director
Application information: No application may be submitted. By nomination from the membership only. Recipients chosen by a committee drawn from the membership and appointed by the Board.

American Academy and Institute of Arts and Letters
633 West 155th Street
New York, NY 10032
(212) 368–5900

Program/Award: The Charles Ives Scholarships; The Charles Ives Fellowship
Description: Annual scholarships to young composers for continued study in composition; annual fellowship to composer.
Restrictions: N/A
Type of art: Composition
$ given: $5,000 per scholarship; $10,000 per fellowship
Number of awards: 6 scholarships per year; 1 fellowship per year
Contact: Lydia Kaim, Assistant to Executive Director

Application information: No applications may be submitted. By nomination from the membership only.

American Academy and Institute of Arts and Letters
633 West 155th Street
New York, NY 10032
(212) 368–5900

Program/Award: The Richard Rodgers Production Award; The Goddard Lieberson Fellowships
Description: The Rodgers Award subsidizes a production in New York of a musical play by authors and composers who are not already established in this field (chosen by a committee of composers and writers appointed by the Board). Staged readings and workshops may be given in lieu of or in addition to the production. The Lieberson Fellowships are given annually to one or two young composers of extraordinary gifts (chosen by a committee of composers).
Restrictions: N/A
Type of art: Composition, Theater
$ given: Rodgers Award varies widely, according to costs of production; Lieberson Fellowships, $10,000 each
Number of awards: 1 Rodgers Award annually; 1–2 Lieberson Fellowships annually
Contact: Lydia Kaim, Assistant to Executive Director
Application information: Rodgers Award application may be obtained by writing to the Academy. Recipients are chosen by a committee drawn from the membership and assisted by experts in the field. No application may be made for the Lieberson Fellowships.

American Accordion Musicological Society
334 South Broadway
Pitman, NJ 08071
(609) 854–6628

Program/Award: Composition Contest

Description: Annual composition contest to foster new works featuring the accordion.

Restrictions: Composer must be acquainted with the various types of accordions.

Type of art: Composition

$ given: $100 to $500 per award annually

Number of awards: N/A

Contact: Stanley Darrow, Secretary

Application information: Write for information.

The American Bandmasters Association
110 Wyanoke Drive
San Antonio, TX 78209
(512) 829–5555

Program/Award: ABA/Ostwald Band Composition Award

Description: Prize with cash award and performance of winning composition by the United States Army Band.

Restrictions: Entries must be original, unpublished compositions for concert band, composed within the last 2 years. Compositions must be conceived and constructed to be playable by professional, university, and high school bands. No time limit on length. Compositions must be submitted with full score; also include good tape recording. Composer's name must not appear on the score; sealed envelope with composer's name and address should be affixed to the title page of the score. Compositions submitted may not be performed in any concerts of the current convention of the ABA. A composer may win the contest no more than 2 times.

Type of art: Composition

$ given: Varies; $4,500 award for 1990

Number of awards: 1 award annually

Contact: Dr. Charles A. Wiley, Chairman of ABA Contest Committee, 111 Torreon Loop, P.O. Box 1076, Ruidoso, NM 88345 (505) 258–4325

Application information: Direct inquiries and send scores and tapes to Dr. Wiley at the Ruidoso address above.

Deadline: December 31; notification and performance at next ABA convention

American College Theatre Festival
Kennedy Center for the Performing Arts
Washington, DC 20566

Program/Award: ASCAP College Musical Theatre Awards
Description: Award for outstanding achievement in the creation of a work for the musical theater by college and university students.
Restrictions: The musical must be original, created and produced by students at a college or university participating in the American College Theatre Festival.
Type of art: Composition, Music, Playwriting
$ given: First Prize, $1,000 for lyrics, $1,000 for music, $1,000 for book, and $1,000 for the institution producing the musical
Number of awards: 4 First Prize awards per year
Contact: The Producing Director
Application information: Write for guidelines and application forms.
Deadline: March 1

American Guild of Organists
815 Second Avenue, Suite 318
New York, NY 10017
(212) 687-9188

Program/Award: HOLTKAMP/AGO Award in Organ Composition Competition
Description: Biennial competition for works featuring the organ.
Restrictions: Composers must be citizens of the U.S., Canada, or Mexico, not older than 35. Composition must be for organ plus 1–5 other instruments, with a performance time not to exceed 15 minutes. Composition must not be previously published.
Type of art: Composition
$ given: $2,000 First Prize
Number of awards: 1 every other year

Contact: N/A
Application information: Write for guidelines and application form.
Deadline: June 1

American Music Center, Inc.
250 West 54th Street
Suite 300
New York, NY 10019
(212) 247-3121

Program/Award: Margaret Fairbank Jory Copying Assistance Program
Description: Grants to reimburse composers for expenses incurred from extraction and copying of parts for premiere performances.
Restrictions: Composers must be seeking funds for first performance of new original work, according to program guidelines. Work must be at least 10 minutes in length and require 7 or more performers.
Type of art: Composition
$ given: Up to $2,000 per award
Number of awards: Approx. 35 awards annually
Contact: Nancy Clarke, Executive Director
Application information: Write for application form and guidelines.
Deadlines: February 1, May 1, October 1

American Society of Composers, Authors and Publishers Foundation
One Lincoln Plaza
New York, NY 10023
(212) 595-3050

Program/Award: Rudolf Nissim Competition
Description: Prize to composer for best new or previously unperformed symphonic work.
Restrictions: Composer must be a member of ASCAP.
Type of art: Composition

$ given: $5,000 per award plus funds to symphony orchestra that agrees to perform the composition
Number of awards: 1 annually
Contact: Frances Richard, Director, Rudolf Nissim Competition
Application information: Write for details.
Deadline: Approx. December 1

American Society of Composers, Authors and Publishers Foundation
One Lincoln Plaza
New York, NY 10023
(212) 595-3050

Program/Award: Young Composers Competition
Description: Awards to young composers whose original compositions are selected by a panel of judges.
Restrictions: Composers must be under 30 years old as of March 15 of the year of application, and must be U.S. citizens or permanent residents.
Type of art: Composition
$ given: $500 to $2,500 per prize
Number of awards: At judges' discretion (total of 15 in one recent year)
Contact: Frances Richard, Director, Young Composers Competition
Application information: Further information available upon request.
Deadline: March 15

The Joseph H. Bearns Prize in Music
Department of Music
Columbia University
703 Dodge
New York, NY 10027
(212) 854-3825

Program/Award: The Joseph H. Bearns Prize in Music
Description: Two prizes, usually given annually; one for a composition in one of the larger forms, the other for a composition

in one of the smaller forms. At the discretion of the judges, there may be more than one award in either or both of these categories.

Restrictions: Limited to U.S. citizens between the ages of 18 and 25, inclusive.

Type of art: Composition

$ given: $3,500 per award for larger form; $2,500 per award for smaller form. Prizes to be divided among recipients in case of more than 2 awards in a category.

Number of awards: Minimum of 1 per category

Contact: Secretary, Department of Music, Columbia University

Application information: Instrumental parts are not needed. Score should be accompanied by the following information: composer's name, address, and telephone number; date and place of birth; social security number; information regarding prior studies; title of work submitted and note of public performances, if any; list of compositions to date. A previous winner of the Bearns Prize may compete a second time, but not two years in succession.

Deadline: February 1; notification by May

Broadcast Music, Inc.
BMI Awards to Student Composers
320 West 57th Street
New York, NY 10019
(212) 586–2000

Program/Award: BMI Awards to Student Composers

Description: Awards for original compositions, vocal or instrumental, by student composers.

Restrictions: Applicants must be citizens or permanent residents of countries within the Western hemisphere and must be enrolled in accredited public, private, or parochial secondary school; enrolled in accredited colleges or conservatories of music; or engaged in the private study of music with recognized and established teachers. Applicants may not have reached their 26th birthday by December 31 of the contest year. Entries must be certified as original compositions. In the case of joint compositions, all cowriters must meet eligibility requirements. No entry may have received any prior prize, award, or commission. Maximum of 3 prizes per student in 3 separate years; maximum of 1 entry per student per year.

Type of art: Composition

$ given: Prizes range from $500 to $2,500, and total $15,000 per year. Distribution is at the discretion of the judges.

Number of awards: Varies each year; usually 10–20

Contact: Dr. Barbara A. Petersen, Director, BMI Awards to Student Composers

Application information: Entries are submitted in manuscript form or, for electronic music or graphic works which cannot be adequately represented in score, may be submitted in taped form. No established limitations on length or instrumentation. Entry blanks and detailed information may be requested from Dr. Petersen.

Deadline: February 10

Concours International de Composition Musicale Genève
Maison de la Radio
Case Postale 233
66, boulevard Carl-Vogt
1211 Geneva 8, Switzerland
41 22 29 23 33; Telex: 422170

Description: Biennial international competition for composition, reserved for musical and theatrical works.

Restrictions: Anonymity of candidates assured. Open to composers of all ages and nationalities. Scores of music for orchestra or ballet, with or without argument (argument not part of competition). Must be completely original, unpublished, and never performed, as a whole or in part, in any way or form whatsoever. No duration is prescribed, but duration should be indicated on first page of score. Manuscript should be legible at first sight.

Type of art: Composition

$ given: First Prize is 20,000 Swiss francs plus production on stage or in concert hall; up to 10,000 Swiss francs for Second and Third prizes. Possible special prizes in addition.

Number of awards: Varies; total of 4 prizes in 1987

Contact: Robert Dunand, General Secretary
Application information: Candidates must provide: conductor's full score; if possible, a piano reduction (or voice and piano); if needed, the sung and/or spoken texts; typed text for argument (if there is one) in French, English, German, or Italian; if needed, a tape recording of electronic or concrete music. All documents must be submitted anonymously, bearing no name or signature, but marked with a distinctive 4-figure number. Include sealed envelope marked on outside with same 4-figure number and containing: name, nationality, date of birth, address, photo; signed declaration that work is original, unpublished, and unperformed; and signed declaration that composer holds all rights for arguments and text.
Deadline: September 30, odd-numbered years

Contemporary Music Festival
Department of Music
Indiana State University
Terre Haute, IN 47809
(812) 237-2768 or 237-2771

Program/Award: Competition for Orchestral Compositions
Description: Competition for contemporary orchestra music.
Restrictions: Winners of this competition within the last 5 years are not eligible. No other restrictions.
Type of art: Composition
$ given: Winners receive performance of their new music by the Louisville Orchestra, participation in festival seminars, and honorarium to cover their expenses for the trip to Terre Haute for the festival.
Number of awards: 3 awards for 1985
Contact: Lawrence Leighton Smith, c/o New Music Composition, 609 West Main Street, Louisville, KY 40202
Application information: Submit full orchestral scores (condensed scores not accepted) to Mr. Smith at the Louisville address above. Orchestra: standard orchestration or less (WW 3333, Brass 4331, Timpani plus 3 percussion, piano, harp, and strings). Compositions must be 10–15 minutes. Scores that include soloists or extra instrumentalists will not be consid-

ered. Summary of necessary instrumentation and accurate timing should be included. A cassette or open-reel (½ track, 7 ½ ips) tape may be submitted with score. Large, neat, and proofread parts must be available upon request. Nonreturnable entry fee of $20 per composer, payable to Louisville Orchestra. Enclose SASE for return of scores not performed.
Deadline: March 1

The Fargo–Moorhead Symphony Orchestra Association
810 Fourth Avenue South
Moorhead, MN 56560
(218) 233–8397

Program/Award: Sigvald Thompson Composition Award
Description: Biennial cash award and premiere performance for an orchestral composition of medium length by an American composer.
Restrictions: Limited to U.S. citizens. Previous winners of this contest not eligible. Manuscript must be of medium length (8–15 minutes), written or completed during the past 2 years, not publicly performed. Scoring for standard symphonic or chamber orchestra without soloists. Choral or solo works not considered.
Type of art: Composition
$ given: $2,000 per award plus performance by the Fargo–Moorhead Symphony Orchestra
Number of awards: 1 award biennially
Contact: The Fargo–Moorhead Symphony, P.O. Box 1753, Fargo, ND 58107–1753
Application information: Submit manuscript with cover sheet listing: name of composition; statement that it has not been publicly performed; name, address, and phone number of composer. Composer's name is not to appear on actual manuscript.
Deadline: September 30, even-numbered years; notification the following spring

Fromm Music Foundation at Harvard
Department of Music
Harvard University
Cambridge, MA 02138
(617) 495-2791

Description: Commissions and grants-in-aid to support composers and performers.
Restrictions: Full-time students not eligible for grants.
Type of art: Composition, Performance—Instrumental
$ given: N/A
Number of awards: N/A
Contact: Earle Brown, Director, 1927 N. Milwaukee Avenue, Chicago, IL 60647-4320
Application information: Individuals and groups may initiate application process by sending résumé and proposal to Mr. Brown at the Chicago address above. No scores should be sent until requested. Requests for supporting materials (e.g. scores and/or tapes) should be sent to David Gable, c/o Department of Music, University of Chicago, 5845 S. Elm Avenue, Chicago, IL 60637.
Deadline: None

John F. Kennedy Center for the Performing Arts
Washington, DC 20566
(202) 872-0466

Program/Award: Kennedy Center Friedheim Awards
Description: Annual awards for new musical compositions.
Restrictions: Composer must be U.S. citizen or resident. Work must be at least 15 minutes in length, be scored for 1–13 instruments, and not include voice, except in the context of musical composition without text.
Type of art: Composition
$ given: Prizes for larger compositions: $5,000 First Place; $2,500 Second Place; $1,000 Third Place; $500 Fourth Place. For smaller compositions: $2,000.
Number of awards: 4 per year

Contact: N/A

Application information: Works may be nominated by anyone, including the composer. Write for complete guidelines and application form.

Deadline: July 15

Musical Prize Contest "Queen Marie-Jose"
Merlinge
CH—1251 GY/Geneva, Switzerland

Description: Biennial prize for a musical composition; instrumentation and time of execution are strictly specified. Subject chosen by the Contest Committee each year.

Restrictions: Open to composers of all nationalities, without age limit.

Type of art: Composition

$ given: 10,000 Swiss francs per award

Number of awards: 1 award every other year

Contact: Secretariat

Application information: All works submitted must be previously unpublished. Clearly legible scores, preferably written in ink, together with a tape recording of the work or a tape recording or an arrangement for piano or for any musical group at the choice of the composer, are to be submitted either to the Contest Secretariat at the address above or to Radio-Television Suisse Romande, Studio de Geneve (66 boulevard Carl-Vogt, 1211 Geneva 8).

Deadline: May 31, even-numbered years; notification the following November

Note: Award-winning work will remain its author's exclusive property.

National Academy of Songwriters
6381 Hollywood Boulevard
Suite 780
Hollywood, CA 90028
(213) 463–7178

Program/Award: American Song Festival

Description: Cash awards and gifts of musical equipment for best new songs.

Restrictions: Open to residents of the U.S. and Canada. Each entry is evaluated by a panel of music business professionals, including songwriters, record producers, music publishers, and representatives from major record companies.

Type of art: Composition

$ given: N/A

Number of awards: N/A

Contact: Coordinator, American Song Festival

Application information: Submit song on standard cassette tape only; one song per cassette, recorded at the beginning of the tape and rewound for judging. Write for additional information.

Deadline: To be announced

Note: This organization was formerly known as Songwriters Resources & Services.

National Association of Composers
P.O. Box 49652
Barrington Station
Los Angeles, CA 90049

Program/Award: Young Composers Competition

Description: Annual competition for young composers.

Restrictions: Composers must be between the ages of 18 and 30, and members of National Association of Composers/USA. Compositions must be for 5 or fewer players and may not be more than 15 minutes in length. Works must be previously unpublished, and may not have won any previous competitions.

Type of art: Composition

$ given: First Prize of $200 plus guaranteed performance; Second Prize of $50 plus guaranteed performance

Number of awards: 2 annually

Contact: N/A

Application information: Write for guidelines and application forms.

Deadline: March 1

National Endowment for the Arts
Music Program
1100 Pennsylvania Avenue, NW
Washington, DC 20506
(202) 682–5445

Program/Award: Composers Program
Description: Composers Fellowships/Collaborative Fellowships
to encourage the creation of new compositions and the completion of works-in-progress, and to generally assist professional development.
Restrictions: Funds are available to composers and their collaborators, such as librettists, video artists, filmmakers, poets, and choreographers. Grants are also available to music performing organizations to enable them to engage a composer-in-residence.
Type of art: Composition
$ given: Up to $25,000 per Composer Fellowship; up to $35,000 per Collaborative Fellowship
Number of awards: N/A
Contact: N/A
Application information: Write for application guidelines and forms.
Deadline: N/A

National Federation of Music Clubs
1336 North Delaware Street
Indianapolis, IN 46202
(317) 638–4003

Program/Award: NFMC Scholarships and Awards
Description: Scholarships and awards for students and adults who show proficiency in the fields of voice, instrumental performance, dance, composition, etc.
Restrictions: In most cases, applicants must be members of the NFMC.
Type of art: Composition, Dance, Performance—Instrumental/Vocal

$ given: $50 to $5,000 per scholarship/award, possibly including performance at NFMC concerts and conventions
Number of awards: N/A
Contact: Patricia M. Midgley, Executive Secretary
Application information: Write for application forms and information. Enclose SASE and $1 for material and handling.
Deadline: Varies

Omaha Symphony Guild
c/o Omaha Symphony Association
310 Aquila Court
Omaha, NE 68102
(402) 342-3836

Program/Award: Omaha Symphony Guild New Music Competition
Description: Cash prize and optional performance of winning work by the Omaha Symphony Chamber Orchestra.
Restrictions: No age limit; open to all composers. No composer may win in 2 consecutive years.
Type of art: Composition
$ given: $2,000 per award
Number of awards: 1 annually
Contact: Donna Rausch, 904 S. 86th Street, Omaha, NE 68114 (402) 397-0993
Application information: Current application forms available on request. Work submitted must be unpublished and must not have been performed by a professional orchestra. $25 entry fee.
Deadline: May 15; notification in December

Pittsburgh New Music Ensemble, Inc.
Duquesne University School of Music
Pittsburgh, PA 15282
(412) 261-0554

Program/Award: Harvey Gaul Composition Contest

Description: Biennial contest (even-numbered years) to promote new music.

Restrictions: Composers must be U.S. citizens. Compositions must not have been published or performed.

Type of art: Composition

$ given: First Prize of $1,500 plus premiere performance by Pittsburgh New Music Ensemble. Honorable mentions will be considered for performance. All works performed will be taped for broadcast.

Number of awards: 1 every other year

Contact: David Stock, Conductor

Application information: Write for application form. Each composition must be signed with a nom de plume.

Deadline: N/A

Also see: American Academy and Institute of Arts and Letters/
FICTION
American Academy in Rome/ARCHITECTURE
Institute of International Education, Cintas/PRINT-
MAKING
National Endowment for the Arts, Jazz/PERFOR-
MANCE—INSTRUMENTAL
National Institute for Music Theatre/PERFOR-
MANCE—VOCAL

Performance—Instrumental

Affiliate Artists Inc.
37 West 65th Street
New York, NY 10023
(212) 580-2000

Program/Award: Affiliate Artists Conductors Program

Description: Program that places gifted young conductors in full-season residencies with major symphony orchestras, to develop the conductors' potential to be future Music Directors.

Restrictions: Applicants must be young, professionally experienced conductors.

Type of art: Music Performance—Conducting
$ given: $1,000 per week plus expenses
Number of awards: 12 for 1990
Contact: Director, Publicity, Advertising, Promotions
Application information: Call or write for application packet.

Affiliate Artists Inc.
37 West 65th Street
New York, NY 10023
(212) 580–2000

Program/Award: Xerox Pianists Program
Description: Program places young pianists in residencies with American symphony orchestras, to perform solo recitals, concert performances, and community residencies (such as senior citizens' homes or hospitals).
Restrictions: Applicants must be professionally experienced pianists.
Type of art: Music Performance
$ given: $1,000 per week plus expenses
Number of awards: 5 for 1990
Contact: Director, Publicity, Advertising, Promotions
Application information: Call or write for application packet.

American Federation of Musicians
1501 Broadway, Suite 600
New York, NY 10036
(212) 869–1330

Program/Award: Lester Petrillo Fund
Description: Emergency fund for disabled musicians who are unable to perform.
Restrictions: Applicants must be members of the American Federation of Musicians.
Type of art: Music Performance
$ given: Varies according to individual needs
Number of awards: Varies
Contact: N/A

Application information: Contact local AMF office for details.
Deadline: None; ongoing funding

American Guild of Organists
475 Riverside Drive, Suite 1260
New York, NY 10115
(212) 870–2310

Program/Award: National Young Artists Competition in Organ
   Performance
Description: Organ-playing competition held at the National Biennial Convention in even-numbered years. Regional competitions select 9 winners and pay their travel expenses to national competition, where 3 national winners are chosen.
Restrictions: Applicants must be under 32 years of age at the time
   of the national competition; must have won local (chapter)
   level and regional competition to be eligible for national com-
   petition.
Type of art: Music Performance
$ given: Prizes are awarded to the 9 regional winners; amounts
   vary. At national level: First Prize of $2,000 (Lilian Murtagh
   Memorial Award); Second Prize of $1,000; Third Prize of
   $500. Performance at National Convention for 3 winners.
Number of awards: 3 national winners every other year
Contact: Philip E. Baker, Director, National Young Artists in
   Organ Performance
Application information: Send request for application form and
   rules to National Headquarters at address above.
Deadline: Varies; write for information.

American Music Scholarship Association
1826 Carew Tower
Cincinnati, OH 45202
(513) 421–5342

Program/Award: International Piano Competition; Artists in
   Residence; Educational Training and Evaluations
Description: Scholarships and debut in New York's Alice Tully
   Hall for piano prodigies and artists.

Restrictions: Student must apply through teacher, who must be a member of AMSA.
Type of art: Music Performance
$ given: $50 to $500 per award; Alice Tully Hall debut
Number of awards: 100 awards for 1985
Contact: Gloria Ackerman, Executive Director
Application information: Write to request student and teacher applications.
Deadline: January 30

American Symphony Orchestra
161 West 54th Street, Suite 1202
New York, NY 10019
(212) 581–1365

Program/Award: Grants Fellowships
Description: Annual competition for young conductors.
Restrictions: Applicants must be U.S. citizens age 35 or younger; must be available for competition and American Symphony Orchestra engagement.
Type of art: Music Performance—Conducting
$ given: First Prize of $5,000; three finalists receive $2,000 each
Number of awards: 4 each year
Contact: N/A
Application information: Write for guidelines, competition dates, and application form.

Augusta Symphony Orchestra
P.O. Box 3684
Augusta, GA 30904

Program/Award: William S. Boyd Piano Competition
Description: Annual performance competition for young pianists.
Restrictions: Pianists must be ages 18–30 and must play the required repertoire.
Type of art: Music Performance
$ given: First Prize of $5,000; Second Prize of $3,000; Third Prize of $2,000

Number of awards: 3 each year
Contact: Mrs. Leland Stoddard, Executive Secretary
Application information: Write for guidelines, list of required pieces, and application form.

Johann Sebastian Bach International Competition
1211 Potomac Street, NW
Washington, DC 20007
(202) 338–1111

Description: Competition to give young artists the opportunity to perform the music of J. S. Bach.
Restrictions: Contestants must be able to perform from memory "The Well-Tempered Clavier," Books I and II.
Type of art: Music Performance
$ given: First place, $4,000; second place, $2,000; third place $1,000
Number of awards: 3 awards per competition
Contact: N/A
Application information: Further information may be obtained from address above. Enclose SASE.

Gina Bachauer International Piano Competition
225 North State Street
Salt Lake City, UT 84103
(801) 521–9200

Description: Triennial international piano competition to encourage young artists.
Restrictions: Open to pianists of any nationality.
Type of art: Music Performance
$ given: Prizes, performance engagements, and support monies, worth over $100,000; distributed among 6 winners
Number of awards: 6 awards every 3 years
Contact: Dr. Paul C. Pollei, Director, GBIPC, P.O. Box 11664, Salt Lake City, UT 84147
Application information: Write for application information. Ap-

plication materials were available after October 1989 for the 1991 award. Application by live audition or dossier and audio tape.

Deadline: Write for information; for 1991 award, application was due one month prior to 1990 live audition, or January 1, 1991, for dossier and audio tape. Notification was June 1991.

F. Busoni International Piano Competition
c/o Conservatorio Statale di Musica "C. Monteverdi"
Piazza Domenicani, 19
39100 Bolzano, Italy
0471–973579

Description: Monetary prize and 50 concert contracts for the winner of this annual piano competition.
Restrictions: Pianists of any nationality, under age 32, are eligible.
Type of art: Music Performance
$ given: 10,000,000 lire First Prize; 5,000,000 lire Second Prize; 4,000,000 lire Third Prize; 3,500,000 lire Fourth Prize; 3,000,000 lire Fifth Prize; 2,500,000 lire Sixth Prize
Number of awards: 6 prizes annually
Contact: Maria Pia Venturi, Secretary
Application information: An official application form must be submitted; write for information.
Deadline: May 31. Competition dates: 2 weeks, August–September

Chamber Music America
545 Eighth Avenue
New York, NY 10018
(212) 244–2772

Program/Award: CMA Residency Program
Description: Direct grants for 1-year residency programs for musicians; planning grants to assist in project development.
Restrictions: Candidates must be an ensemble member in good

standing of CMA; have a minimum of 2 years of continuous public performance and operation; have experience in touring, workshops, or other residency-related activities.

Type of art: Music Performance
$ given: $5,000 to $10,000 per grant; planning grants of $2,500
Number of awards: 12 grants (all types) for the year 1989–90
Contact: Maria Theresa Stadtmueller, Program Director
Application information: Write for guidelines.
Deadline: late winter; notification late spring

Civic Orchestra of Chicago
220 South Michigan Avenue
Chicago, IL 60604
(312) 435–8159

Program/Award: Civic Orchestra of Chicago Soloist Auditions
Description: Payment of honorarium and expenses involved in coming to Chicago to perform with the Civic Orchestra as soloists.
Restrictions: Audition open to persons playing all orchestral instruments and piano who will be at least 19 but not yet 30 by October 1 of the year of audition. Prior Civic soloists not eligible.
Type of art: Music Performance
$ given: $1,000 plus expenses per award
Number of awards: 3 for the year 1988–89
Contact: N/A
Application information: Write for application forms.
Deadline: Approx. March 15

Van Cliburn Foundation, Inc.
2525 Ridgmar Boulevard, Suite 307
Fort Worth, TX 76116
(817) 738–6536

Program/Award: Van Cliburn International Piano Competition
Description: International competition for pianists ready to be

launched on a professional performing and touring career. Competitions are held every 4 years, with the next scheduled for the spring of 1993.

Restrictions: Open to pianists of both sexes and all nationalities, ages 18–30.

Type of art: Music Performance

$ given: Total value of first prize estimated to be in excess of $200,000; includes $15,000 cash prize plus U.S. and Euorpean concert tour; Second Prize: $10,000 plus concert tour; Third Prize, $7,500; Fourth Prize, $5,000; Fifth Prize, $3,500; Sixth Prize, $2,000

Number of awards: 6 every 4 years

Contact: Richard Rodzinski, Executive Director

Application information: Write for information.

Deadline: November 1, 1992, for 1993 competition

Concert Artists Guild, Inc.
850 Seventh Avenue
Suite 1003
New York, NY 10019
(212) 333-5200

Program/Award: Annual International Competition for All Instrumentalists, Vocalists, and Keyboard Players

Description: Career development for emerging artists provided cost-free. Artists chosen are presented in New York and nationwide recitals and are provided with management services that lead to bookings with concert series and orchestras.

Restrictions: Applicants may not have had a formal New York debut. Previous first-place winners may not apply, but second-place winners may. Persons with full-service U.S. management contracts are not eligible.

Type of art: Music Performance—Instrumental/Vocal

$ given: First-place winners receive $2,500 cash prize; recital at a major New York hall; other recitals in cities around the country; free management services for 2 years; a commissioned work written for them; bookings around the country in recital series and with orchestras. Second-place winners receive $500 cash.

Number of awards: Maximum of 3 first-place winners each year (not fixed)

Contact: Ellen Highstein, Executive Director

Application information: Write the Guild office in September for application forms and complete information on procedures.

Deadline: January

Concours Clara Haskil
35, rue du Village
1802 Corseaux/Vevey, Switzerland
(021) 921 30 14; FAX: (021) 922 85 67

Description: Biennial piano competition for young musicians of any nationality.

Restrictions: Pianists of either sex, from any country, age 32 or younger.

Type of art: Music Performance

$ given: First Prize of 12,000 Swiss francs plus concert engagements for broadcast and live performances; 1,000 Swiss francs for each finalist

Number of awards: 1 first-place winner every 2 years

Contact: Nicole Klopfenstein, Director, Concours Clara Haskil, C.P. 17, CH—1802 Corseaux/Vevey, Switzerland

Application information: Write for entry form. Entry fee required.

Deadline: July 5; preliminary judging end of August

Avery Fisher Artist Program
140 West 65th Street
New York, NY 10023
(212) 877–1800

Program/Award: The Avery Fisher Prize; The Avery Fisher Career Grants

Description: Awards for excellence and help in launching young major careers.

Restrictions: Applicants must be U.S. citizens and classical instrumentalists.

Type of art: Music Performance

$ given: Avery Fisher Prize, $25,000; Career Grants, $10,000 each

Number of awards: Avery Fisher Prize considered annually but not necessarily awarded (max. 1 annually); up to 5 Career Grants annually

Contact: N/A

Application information: Individual artists may not apply directly. Nominations are made by the Recommendation Board, which comprises nationally known instrumentalists, conductors, music educators, and presenters. Final selections are made by the Executive Committee. The program is administered by the Lincoln Center for the Performing Arts, Inc.

Folkestone Menuhin International Violin Competition
Kallaway Ltd.
2 Portland Road, Holland Park
London W11 4LA, England
01–221 7883

Description: Annual competition for young violinists.

Restrictions: Participants must be under age 22.

Type of art: Music Performance

$ given: £13,200 total value of prize money

Number of awards: 13 prizes each year

Contact: The Director

Application information: Write for entry form.

Deadline: January; competition and awards, April

Fort Collins Symphony Association
425 West Mulberry Street, Suite 110
Fort Collins, CO 80521
(303) 482–4823

Program/Award: Young Artists Competition

Description: Cash awards to encourage students in music performance. Piano and instrumental divisions.

Restrictions: Junior level, through age 18; Senior level, through age 25.

Type of art: Music Performance

$ given: Senior level, First Prize, $2,000; Second Prize, $500. Junior level, First Prize, $250; Second Prize, $50. Three finalists perform with the orchestra.

Number of awards: 8 awards for 1987

Contact: Paul Batchelor, General Manager, P.O. Box 1963, Fort Collins, CO 80522

Application information: Entry fee of $20 for Senior level, $10 for Junior level. Signature of entrant's music instructor is required for application. Former first-place Senior level winners may not enter again.

Deadline: February 1

Institute of International Education
Arts International Program
809 United Nations Plaza
New York, NY 10017–3580
(212) 883–8200

Program/Award: MUSICA Travel Grants

Description: Travel grants to selected international music competitions to enable the best young American musical talent to participate in international music competitions abroad.

Restrictions: Limited to U.S. citizens. Applicants' talent and professional experience must indicate that they are sufficiently advanced to be contenders in a competition.

Type of art: Music Competition

$ given: Funding to cover costs of travel and, in some instances, precompetition instruction

Number of awards: Varies; 10 grants in 1990

Contact: Rebecca A. Abrams, Associate Program Officer

Application information: Write for application forms. Record of training and performance experience as well as 2 letters of recommendation required with completed application.

Deadline: June 1

International Competition for Musical Performers—Geneva
104, rue de Carouge
1205 Geneva, Switzerland
(022) 28 62 08; FAX: (022) 20 43 66

Program/Award: Geneva International Competition for Musical Performers
Description: Competitive prizes for musical performers. Programs change every year. Categories for 1991: singing, violincello, tuba, organ; for 1992: piano, viola, flute, percussion.
Restrictions: Open to all nationalities. Age limit for all instrumentalists is 30; for male singers, 34; for female singers, 32.
Type of art: Music Performance—Instrumental/Vocal
$ given: 10,000 Swiss francs First Prize in each category; 7,500 Swiss francs Second Prize; 5,000 Swiss francs Third Prize. Special Award: Swiss Prize, 10,000 Swiss francs. Also, broadcasting, TV, and orchestra recital contracts are awarded.
Number of awards: 3 prizes in each category per year; 4 categories per year
Contact: The C.I.E.M. Secretariat
Application information: A prospectus in 3 languages (French, German, and English) is available from the address above. Application fee of 150 Swiss francs is required upon formal application.
Deadline: May 31

International Marguerite Long–Jacques Thibaud Competition
32, avenue Matignon
75008 Paris, France
33 (1) 42 66 66 80

Description: International competition for piano and violin.
Restrictions: Open to musicians of any nationality, between ages 16–30.
Type of art: Music Performance
$ given: 80,000 francs, First Grand Prize
Number of awards: 6 prizes and special prizes per competition
Contact: Chantal Bernard, Secretaire-General
Application information: Future competition schedule: Piano,

1992 and 1995; Violin, 1993 and 1996. Write for deadline and application information.

Montreal International Music Competition
Concours International de Musique de Montreal
Place des Arts
1501, rue Jeanne-Mance
Montreal, PQ H2X 129, Canada
(514) 285–4380

Description: Competition devoted to violin, piano, and voice, scheduled on a 4-year cycle (3 years contest, 1 year recess). Recess years, 1990, 1994. Violin, 1991. Piano, 1992. Voice, 1993.

Restrictions: Applicants must be 16–30 years of age for violin and piano; 20–35 years of age for voice. All nationalities eligible.

Type of art: Music Performance—Instrumental/Vocal

$ given: First Prize of $15,000; Second Prize of $7,500; Third Prize of $3,000; Fourth Prize of $1,500; Fifth Prize of $1,000; four other prizes of $500 each

Number of awards: 9 awards per competition year

Contact: N/A

Application information: Write for application forms. Must be submitted with document certifying birth date and nationality, curriculum vitae, photographs, transcripts, recommendations, performance reviews, list of works to be performed in competition.

Deadline: March 1; notification within 1 month

National Endowment for the Arts
Music Program
1100 Pennsylvania Avenue, NW
Washington, DC 20506
(202) 682–5445

Program/Award: Jazz

Description: Grants to Individuals: funding for professional jazz performers, to support rehearsals, performances, and the preparation of audio and video demo tapes and related expenses; and for professional jazz composers to support the creation of new works, the completion of works-in-progress, and the reproduction of scores of parts of completed works. Fellowships: NEA also offers up to 5 fellowships to distinguished jazz masters. Jazz Special Projects support to individuals for innovative and exemplary projects of national or regional significance that benefit the field of jazz and are not eligible under other jazz funding categories.

Restrictions: See Description.

Type of art: Music Performance, Composition

$ given: $3,000 to $7,500 per Grant to Individual, for performer or composer; up to $20,000 per Jazz Masters fellowship; Special Projects grants range from $5,000 to $10,000 per grant

Number of awards: N/A

Contact: N/A

Application information: Write for guidelines and forms.

National Endowment for the Arts
Music Program
1100 Pennsylvania Avenue, NW
Washington, DC 20506
(202) 682–5445

Program/Award: Music Recording

Description: Matching grants for nonprofit organizations and solo and duo performers for the recording and distribution of American music.

Restrictions: N/A

Type of art: Music Performance

$ given: $5,000 to $20,000 per grant; funds must be matched, 1 to 1

Number of awards: N/A

Contact: N/A

Application information: Write for guidelines and forms.

National Endowment for the Arts
Music Program
1100 Pennsylvania Avenue, NW
Washington, DC 20506
(202) 682–5445

Program/Award: Solo Recitalists
Description: Fellowships to individuals of outstanding talent with the potential for major careers as solo recitalists. Program operates on a 2-year cycle: Fiscal year 1992 fellowships to vocalists and keyboard recitalists; fiscal year 1993 fellowships to all other instrumental recitalists.
Restrictions: N/A
Type of art: Music Performance—Instrumental/Vocal
$ given: $7,500 to $15,000 per fellowship
Number of awards: N/A
Contact: N/A
Application information: Write for guidelines and forms.

Sociedade Brasileira de Realizaçoes Artistico-Culturais
Av. F. Roosevelt 23-S. 310
Rio de Janeiro 22,000, Brazil
551–1468; 275–6456

Program/Award: International Singing Contest (XV) 1991; Piano for Accompanists Contest (III) 1991
Description: International, government-recognized competitions.
Restrictions: Singers must be under age 32. No age limit for accompanists.
Type of art: Music Performance—Instrumental/Vocal
$ given: Medals, engagements in Brazil and abroad, and the following cash prizes: $3,000 Great Prize; $3,000 prize from Ministry of Foreign Affairs; $2,000 prize from Gulbenkian Foundation; $2,000 prize from OEA for Best American Singer; several minor prizes totaling $2,000
Number of awards: Varies; 5 awards for 1987
Contact: Blanca Boucas, Library
Application information: Write for information. Required with

application form: copy of birth certificate, short curriculum vitae, publicity material, copies of diplomas and other awards. **Deadline:** Write for information; in 1991, the deadline was January 1 for the June 10–20, 1991 contest.

University of Maryland International Piano Festival and William Kapell Competition
Summer Programs
University of Maryland
College Park, MD 20742
(301) 405–6544

Program/Award: International Piano Festival and Competition
Description: Prizes for outstanding pianists. Annual competition held in July at the University of Maryland.
Restrictions: Pianists must be age 18–33.
Type of art: Music Performance
$ given: $15,000 First Prize; $10,000 Second Prize; $5,000 Third Prize; plus other special prizes and semifinalist prizes
Number of awards: Approx. 15 each year
Contact: Piano Festival Coordinator
Application information: Prospective contestants must submit completed application form, including the entire program to be performed; confirmation of date and place of birth and nationality; curriculum vitae; $50 registration fee; and a tape of at least 30 minutes (no specific repertoire required).
Deadline: April 1 for May 1 selection of accepted contestants

Also see: Affiliate Artists Inc./PERFORMANCE—VOCAL
Carnegie Hall International/PERFORMANCE—VOCAL
Fondation des Etats-Unis/VISUAL ARTS—GENERAL
Fromm Music Foundation at Harvard/COMPOSITION
National Federation of Music Clubs/COMPOSITION

Performance—Vocal

Affiliate Artists Inc.
37 West 65th Street
New York, NY 10023
(212) 580–2000

Program/Award: Affiliate Artists Residency Program
Description: Program offering residency opportunities for young professionals of all performing arts disciplines in communities throughout the country. Residencies vary in duration, ranging from 1 to 6 weeks. Residencies are sponsored by corporations, foundations, and government agencies.
Restrictions: Applicants must be professionally experienced opera singers, modern dancers, actors, classical and jazz instrumentalists, pianists, and mimes.
Type of art: Music Performance, Dance, Theater
$ given: $1,000 per week plus expenses
Number of awards: 8 for 1990
Contact: Joseph Chart or Susan Haugen
Application information: Solo performing artists are encouraged to call or write for application packet. Artists may participate for up to 5 years.
Deadline: Usually late summer/early fall; national auditions, winter/spring

Baltimore Opera Company, Inc.
527 North Charles Street
Baltimore, MD 21201–5030
(301) 727–0592

Program/Award: Baltimore Opera Annual National Vocal Competition for Operatic Artists
Description: Cash awards and performance contracts to provide substantial career assistance to young American artists of superior potential.
Restrictions: Limited to artists age 20–35.
Type of art: Music Performance
$ given: Awards range from $1,000 to $10,000 each, for the top

7 prizes. Additional special prizes. Each semifinalist not awarded a prize receives a $150 stipend. Prizes are awarded on the condition that funds are used for one or more of the following: to further voice training, to learn operatic roles, to develop dramatic ability, or to perfect foreign languages.

Number of awards: 7 awards total in 1989

Contact: Gary M. Madison

Application information: Applications are obtained from the BOC and should be submitted with evidence of birth and 2 letters of recommendation, along with a $30 nonrefundable registration fee. All auditions must be in person; recordings, of any kind, are unacceptable.

Deadline: Mid-May for finals in June

Concorso Internationale per Voci Verdiane A. e M. Ziliani—Busseto
Viale F. Testi, 76
20126 Milano, Italy
02–6471961

Program/Award: International Competition for Verdian Voices

Description: Cash prizes, scholarships, concerts, opera.

Restrictions: Competition is international, open to singers of all nationalities. Singers of both sexes eligible. For 1990 competition, contestants must have been born after January 1953 if soprano or tenor; after January 1951 if mezzo-soprano, baritone, or bass. No scholastic or musical degree required. Judged by committee solely on performances.

Type of art: Music Performance

$ given: 5,000,000 lire First Prize; 3,000,000 lire Second Prize; 2,000,000 lire Third Prize; plus 6 prizes for participation of singers in the courses of Accademia Verdiana

Number of awards: 10 prizes per competition

Contact: Elio Manzoni, Secretary, Piazza G. Verdi, 10, 43011 Busseto, Italy

Application information: Candidates who intend to participate should return completed application form, copy of birth certificate, photocopy of identity card or passport, 2 identity-card-size photos, and enrollment fee of 50,000 lire by means

of bank draft. Nonpayment of fee automatically excludes candidate from competition. Fee in no case reimbursable.
Deadline: May 31

Concours International de Chant de la Ville de Toulouse
Theatre du Capitole
Place du Capitole
31000 Toulouse, France
61 23 21 35; Telex: 530.891

Program/Award International Voice Competition of Toulouse
Description: Competition with cash awards. Singers must present 12 pieces: 6 in Group 1, oratorio or art songs or lieder (1 by French composer); 6 in Group 2, arias from opera, comic opera, or operetta (1 aria by French composer). All performed in the original language.
Restrictions: All nationalities eligible. Contestants must be age 18–33.
Type of art: Music Performance
$ given: First Prize, 20,000 FF each for male and female categories; Second Prize, 10,000 FF each for male and female categories; Third Prize, 5,000 FF each for male and female categories. Special prizes of 5,000 FF and 2,500 FF.
Number of awards: 10 awards per competition
Contact: Monsieur Georges Canet, Secretaire General du Concours International de Chant
Application information: Candidates must submit application form, birth certificate, 3 photos, clear account of artistic achievements.
Deadline: Mid-September for one-week competition in October

Detroit Grand Opera Association
500 Temple Avenue
Detroit, MI 48201
(313) 832–5200

Program/Award: Opera Scholarships and Awards

Description: Cash grants for musical performers.

Restrictions: Write for information on age and residency limitations.

Type of art: Music Performance

$ given: $3,000 Samuel B. Lang Opera Scholarship; $1,000 Elizabeth Hodges Donovan Memorial Award; $1,000 Henry E. Wenger Memorial Award; $1,500 Francis Robinson Memorial Award

Number of awards: 3–4 per year

Contact: N/A

Application information: Write for details.

Deadline: October; notification in mid-November

Illinois Opera Guild
Auditions of the Air
DePaul University School of Music
804 West Belden Avenue
Chicago, IL 60614–3214
(312) 362–8373

Program/Award: Auditions of the Air

Description: Nationwide competition for young operatic vocal artists.

Restrictions: Open to U.S. citizens, male and female, 20–33 as of May of the year of competition. Contestants must reside in the U.S. or its possessions. Open to professional and nonprofessional singers who have completed, or are engaged in completing, a suitable musical education for the operatic stage and who have not made an operatic debut in a leading role with a major opera company. Winners must use the award to further their careers.

Type of art: Music Performance

$ given: First Award of $5,000 plus solo appearance in one of Chicago's Grant Park Summer Concerts; Second Award of $2,000; honorable mentions totaling $1,000

Number of awards: At least 2 awards per competition

Contact: Adele Szymanski, Executive Director, Auditions of the Air

Application information: Submit recording of voice together with official application blank to Auditions Committee. Request further information and application blanks from the address above.

Deadline: April 1, with auditions in mid-June

International Vocal Competition's-Hertogenbosch
Parade 19
5211 KL 's-Hertogenbosch, The Netherlands
073–136569

Description: Competition for solo singing in the categories of opera, oratorio, and lied.

Restrictions: Open to singers of all voice categories and nationalities. Outstanding vocal and artistic qualities required. Applicants for 1990 competition had to have been born after December 31, 1957.

Type of art: Music Performance

$ given: First Prizes, Dfl 10,000 for each category (opera, oratorio, lied); Second Prizes, Dfl 5,000 for each voice; Erna Spoorenberg Award, Dfl 3,000 for opera; Elly Ameling Award, Dfl 3,000 for lied; Dutch Music Award, Dfl 5,000 for best performance of Dutch repertoire; plus various other cash prizes. Finals are played with orchestra and broadcast on radio and TV.

Number of awards: 10 prizes in 1988

Contact: Marijke Roef, Director

Application information: Write for application form. Entry fee of Dfl 160.

Metropolitan Opera National Council
Lincoln Center
New York, NY 10023
(212) 799-3100

Program/Award: Metropolitan Opera National Council Competition

Description: Auditions to discover new talent for the operatic world and encourage and assist talented young singers in furthering their careers. Winners of 17 regional auditions in the U.S., Canada, and Australia go to New York City to be coached by the Metropolitan Opera artistic staff and compete in national finals; national winners receive cash and performance with the Met company in an annual winners' concert.

Restrictions: The use of funds is limited to educational expenses, specifically those incurred to train and perfect the singer's voice, style, acting, and languages.

Type of art: Music Performance

$ given: Regional winners receive the Tobin Award and $400; runners-up receive the Brush Memorial Award and $200 or $300. Regional winners compete in national finals in New York. Finalists receive $1,000; the winner receives $10,000 and performs in the National Council's Annual Winners' Concert at the Met, accompanied by the Metropolitan Opera company.

Number of awards: 17 regional winners; 9–11 finalists; 1 national winner

Contact: Lawrence F. Stayce, Executive Director of Auditions

Application information: Write for guidelines.

Deadline: Varies from region to region

National Association of Composers
P.O. Box 49652
Barrington Station
Los Angeles, CA 90049

Program/Award: Young Performers Competition

Description: Annual competition for performers of works by 20th-century composers.

Restrictions: Contestants must be age 18–30. Repertoire must include at least 2 compositions by 20th-century composers, representing a variety of styles, either solo or with piano.

Type of art: Music Performance

$ given: $200 plus possible performance

Number of awards: N/A

Contact: N/A
Application information: Write for guidelines and application forms. Submit cassette tape recording of 15–25 minutes of the required repertoire with completed application form.
Deadline: March 1

National Association of Teachers of Singing, Inc.
2800 University Boulevard North
Jacksonville, FL 32211
(904) 744–9022

Program/Award: Artist Awards
Description: Awards to select young singers (age 21–35) ready to embark on professional careers, and to encourage these young artists to carry on the tradition of fine singing as professional artists. Selection made on present accomplishment rather than on potential.
Restrictions: Applicant's most recent teacher must be a NATS National member in good standing; applicant must have studied with NATS teacher continuously for at least 1 year; applicants must be between 21 and 35 as of deadline entry date; NATS members in good standing for at least 1 year prior to deadline date are eligible; first-place winners may not compete again.
Type of art: Music Performance
$ given: First Place $5,000; Second Place $2,500; Third Place $1,500; and $500 to each of the other 11 regional winners at National Convention
Number of awards: 14 awards per competition. Awards presented in NATS convention years at 18-month intervals.
Contact: Jay Wilkey, NATSAA Coordinator, 2825 Lexington Road, Louisville, KY 40280–1934
Application information: Write for application forms. Applicant must enter district or state auditions nearest legal residence or place where studying voice. (Send application directly to National Coordinator. Applicants will be informed of date and location of preliminary auditions.) Contestants progress from state to regional to semifinal to final competition levels.

National Institute for Music Theater
John F. Kennedy Center for the Performing Arts
Washington, DC 20566

Program/Award: George London Grants for Singers; Fellowships in Composition (as well as Project Grants for Singers and Singer Contract Support)
Description: Direct grants to young opera and musical theater singers; fellowship program for creators and their immediate collaborators (e.g., stage and music directors, coach/accompanists).
Restrictions: N/A
Type of art: Music Performance, Composition
$ given: $2,000 to $20,000 per singer for London Grants; up to $20,000 per Fellowship in Composition
Number of awards: Varies; 11 London Grants in 1988; 8 Fellowships in 1988
Contact: Program Director
Application information: Guidelines appear in summer. Write for application guidelines and forms.
Deadline: Varies with each program

National Opera Association, Inc.
Route 2, Box 196
Commerce, TX 75428
(214) 886-3830

Program/Award: Student and Artist Auditions
Description: Cash prizes awarded to Artist Division winners; cash prizes to school, voice teacher, or vocal coach of Scholarship Division winners.
Restrictions: All winners must be members of NOA. Individual memberships available for $30.
Type of art: Music Performance
$ given: $250 to $1,000 per award
Number of awards: N/A
Contact: Mary Elaine Wallace, Executive Secretary
Application information: Write for information. Ask for deadline and contest dates.

New Jersey State Opera
1020 Broad Street
Newark, NJ 07102
(201) 623–5757 or 623–5758

Description: Regional scholarship auditions, possible contract with NJSO.
Restrictions: Applicants must be age 22–34, and must demonstrate evidence of serious commitment to the pursuit of opera as a career. No geographic limitations.
Type of art: Music Performance
$ given: 4 $1,000 awards; 1 $2,500 Puccini Foundation Award
Number of awards: 5 per year
Contact: Mrs. Barbara Burke, Director, Auditions Program
Application information: 2 written recommendations are required, as is a birth certificate or other proof of age.
Deadline: Usually spring, with notification in January

Orchestra League of Oklahoma City
2424 N.W. 113th
Oklahoma City, OK 73120
(405) 752–5196

Program/Award: The Steward Awards
Description: National biennial juried competition with cash awards and performance with the Oklahoma Symphony Orchestra. All major opera companies will be notified of winners. Videotapes of finals available for viewing. Judges are nationally known performers, directors, and teachers in the field of opera.
Restrictions: Open to all categories of singers who are U.S. citizens age 20–32 as of March the year of the award.
Type of art: Music Performance
$ given: $5,000 First Place; $2,500 Second Place; $1,000 Third Place; plus 3 awards of $500 each
Number of awards: 6 awards per competition
Contact: Mrs. Donald Jensen, Chairman, The Stewart Awards, P.O. Box 13188, Oklahoma City, OK 73113, (405) 752-5196
Application information: Write for application form. No en-

dorsements required. Application must be accompanied by videotape with required repertoire.

Deadline: November 1, 1991, for videotape preliminaries; March 1992 finals

Richard Tucker Music Foundation
277 West End Avenue, Suite 11A
New York, NY 10023
(212) 496–5154

Program/Award: Richard Tucker Award; Career Grants; Robert M. Jacobson Study Grants; Opera Company Grants; Sara Tucker Distinguished Service Award
Description: Financial aid to American opera singers and opera companies with development programs for American singers.
Restrictions: Students are not eligible. Applicants must already be performing in opera. Open to males and females in all categories.
Type of art: Music Performance
$ given: $25,000 per Richard Tucker Award; $5,000 per Career Grant; $5,000 per Study Grant; $10,000 per Company Grant; $5,000 per Sara Tucker Distinguished Service Award
Number of awards: Distribution in 1989, 1 Richard Tucker Award, 4 Career Grants, 2 Study Grants, 1 Company Grant, 1 Sara Tucker Award
Contact: Karen K. Nelson, Executive Director
Application information: Singers may not apply; they must be recommended by a recognized professional in the field.
Deadline: December 1, with notification in late spring

The Loren L. Zachary Society for the Performing Arts
2250 Gloaming Way
Beverly Hills, CA 90210
(213) 276–2731

Program/Award: Annual Opera Awards National Vocal Competition
Description: Annual competition to promote and discover new

operatic talent, making it possible for young singers to obtain gainful employment in their profession.

Restrictions: Singers must be age 21–33, have completed proper operatic training, and be prepared to pursue professional stage careers.

Type of art: Music Performance

$ given: 2 winners receive $3,000 each plus round-trip airfare to Europe for auditions; remaining awards are $1,000 each.

Number of awards: 10 awards for 1989

Contact: Nedra Zachary, Director of Auditions

Application information: Submit letter requesting information and application in January. Singers must be present in either Los Angeles or New York for all phases of auditions; tapes not acceptable. Requests for applications must be accompanied by SASE (#10 size).

Deadline: February/March, varies each year. Final auditions are in Pasadena, California, in May.

Also see: Concert Artists Guild/PERFORMANCE—INSTRU-
MENTAL

International Competition for Musical Performers—
Geneve/PERFORMANCE—INSTRUMENTAL

Montreal International Music Competition/PERFOR-
MANCE—INSTRUMENTAL

National Endowment for the Arts, Solo Recitalists/
PERFORMANCE—INSTRUMENTAL

National Federation of Music Clubs/COMPOSITION

Sociedade Brasileira de Realizacoes Artistico-Cul-
turais/PERFORMANCE—INSTRUMENTAL

Theater

Performance Art

Art Matters
P.O. Box 1428
New York, NY 10011
(212) 929-7190

Program/Award: Awards to Individuals
Description: Funds to aid individual artists in ongoing, unrestricted, project-specific visual art work and performance work with a strong visual emphasis.
Restrictions: Emphasis on experimental art.
Type of art: Visual Art, Performance Art, Multimedia Installation, Artists' Books
$ given: $1,000 to $5,000 per grant
Number of grants: Approx. 41 per year
Contact: Laura Donnelly, President; Marianne Weems, Administrator
Application information: Write to request application form.
Deadline: N/A; notification within 2 months of application

National Endowment for the Arts
Theater Program
1100 Pennsylvania Avenue, NW
Washington, DC 20506
(202) 682–5425

Program/Award: Fellowships for Mimes and Solo Performing Artists
Description: Grants to exceptionally talented professional individual artists working independently of companies and exploring new styles and forms of theater, including puppetry. Financial assistance for activities that contribute to an individual's artistic growth.
Restrictions: N/A
Type of art: Performance Art
$ given: $5,000 to $12,500 per award

Number of awards: N/A
Contact: Grants Office/Theater
Application information: Write for application guidelines, forms, and deadline information.

Also see: Affiliate Artists Inc./MUSIC PERFORMANCE—
VOCAL
National Endowment for the Arts, Visual Arts/VI-
SUAL ARTS—GENERAL

Playwriting

Academy of Motion Picture Arts and Sciences
8949 Wilshire Boulevard
Beverly Hills, CA 90211–1972
(213) 278-8990

Program/Award: The Don and Gee Nicholl Fellowships in Screenwriting
Description: Fellowships to provide living expenses for one year, roughly December 1 to November 30, for promising new writers so that they may concentrate exclusively for that period on writing for the screen. Not for collaborative efforts.
Restrictions: Limited to legal residents of the U.S. who have not worked as professional screenwriters for theatrical films or TV or sold screen or TV rights to an original story, treatment, screenplay, or teleplay. During the fellowship year, Nicholl Fellows are expected to complete an original screenplay (100–130 pages) written in standard screenplay format. Nicholl Fellowships may not be held concurrently with other fellowships. Fellows are expected to devote all working time to writing.
Type of art: Screenwriting
$ given: $20,000 per fellowship, payable quarterly over one year; installments subject to satisfactory progress of work, according to the Academy's Nicholl Fellowship Committee
Number of awards: Up to 5 annually, but the Academy reserves the right to grant no award if the Committee judges no application to be of sufficient merit

Contact: Julian Blaustein, Chairman, Nicholl Fellowship Committee

Application information: Applicants must submit 2 copies of an original screenplay for a feature-length film. Individual work only. Submissions may not be based, in whole or in part, on any other fictional material—published or unpublished, produced or unproduced. Application forms, completed in entirety, must accompany submissions. Applications accepted only by mail. Submissions cannot be returned.

Deadline: June 1, with notification in mid-November

Actors Theatre of Louisville
316–320 West Main Street
Louisville, KY 40202
(502) 584–1265

Program/Award: The Great American Play Contest

Description: Competition for one-act and full-length original plays.

Restrictions: Limited to U.S. citizens. Plays submitted may not have had previous Equity productions or Equity waivers.

Type of art: Playwriting

$ given: $7,500 to best full-length play; $1,000 to best one-act play. Winning plays are considered for production by the Actors Theatre of Louisville.

Number of awards: 1 per category

Contact: Literary Manager

Application information: Write for guidelines and application form.

Deadline: April 15

American Academy and Institute of Arts and Letters
633 West 155th Street
New York, NY 10032
(212) 368-5900

Program/Award: Award of Merit Medal

Description: Award to honor distinguished artists, composers, and writers who are not members of the Academy. Conferred

for work of distinction with the purpose of furthering literature and the fine arts and stimulating and encouraging the arts
in the U.S.

Restrictions: Recipients must be U.S. citizens or residents who
are not members of the Academy.

Type of art: Fiction, Playwriting, Poetry, Sculpture, Painting

$ given: N/A

Number of awards: N/A

Contact: N/A

Application information: Applications are not accepted; nomination by members of the Academy only.

American College Theatre Festival
Kennedy Center for the Performing Arts
Washington, DC 20566

Program/Award: ASCAP College Musical Theatre Awards

Description: Award for outstanding achievement in the creation
of a work for the musical theater by college and university
students.

Restrictions: The original student musical must be produced by
a college or university participating in the American College
Theatre Festival.

Type of art: Composition, Playwriting

$ given: First Prize, $1,000 for lyrics; $1,000 for music; $1,000 for
book; and $1,000 to the institution producing the musical

Number of awards: 4 awards to the first-place musical production

Contact: The Producing Director

Application information: Write for guidelines and application
forms.

Deadline: March 1

American College Theatre Festival
Kennedy Center for the Performing Arts
Washington, DC 20566

Program/Award: Jane Chambers Playwriting Award

Description: Award for a new play in which the central character and the majority of principal roles are women. Application by female playwrights is especially encouraged.

Restrictions: Only previously unproduced scripts entered in the American College Theatre Festival are eligible.

Type of art: Playwriting

$ given: $500 and a reading of the winning play at the national convention of the American Theatre Association

Number of awards: 1 per year

Contact: The Producing Director

Application information: Write for guidelines, application form, and deadline information.

**American College Theatre Festival
Kennedy Center for the Performing Arts
Washington, DC 20566**

Program/Award: The David Library of the American Revolution Awards

Description: Awards to student writers and college theaters for full-length plays on the broad subject of American freedom.

Restrictions: Plays must be performed as part of the American College Theatre Festival, produced by a college or university, and written by students. Colleges may produce plays by students other than their own.

Type of art: Playwriting

$ given: First Prize of $2,000; Second Prize of $1,000

Number of awards: 2 per year

Contact: The Producing Director

Application information: Write for guidelines and application forms.

Deadline: October 15

**American College Theatre Festival
Kennedy Center for the Performing Arts
Washington, DC 20566**

Program/Award: Lorraine Hansberry Award

Description: Award for best play on the black experience in

America, of those entered in the Student Playwriting Program of the Festival.

Restrictions: Plays must be written by a student and produced by a college or university.

Type of art: Playwriting

$ given: First Prize of $2,500 for playwright and $750 for drama department of producing college or university; Second Prize of $1,000 to playwright

Number of awards: 3 per year

Contact: The Producing Director

Application information: Write for guidelines and application form.

Deadline: October 30

The Beverly Hills Theatre Guild
Box 148
Beverly Hills, CA 90213
(213) 273–3033

Program/Award: The Beverly Hills Theatre Guild–Julie Harris Playwright Award Competition

Description: Annual cash awards to 3 American playwrights whose submitted plays earn the vote of independent professional evaluators for the awards.

Restrictions: Limited to U.S. citizens. Play must have a minimum 90-minute playing time; must be unproduced, unpublished, and not previously entered in this competition; must not have won any other major competitions. Adaptations, translations, and musicals are not eligible.

Type of art: Playwriting

$ given: First Prize, $5,000 to playwright plus $2,000 to help finance a showcase production of the play, if produced in the Los Angeles area within one year of receipt of award; Second Prize, $1,000; Third Prize, $500

Number of awards: 3 awards per year

Contact: Marcella Meharg, Playwright Award Coordinator, 2815 North Beachwood Drive, Los Angeles, CA 90068

Application information: All applicants should send for contest rules before applying to ensure eligibility and to receive the

required application form. Requests for information should be accompanied by SASE. Playwright must personally sign the application; manuscript must be bound and contain a cast list, number of sets, acts, and scenes; include 2 title pages, 1 without the author's name bound to the script, the other with name clipped to front of script.
Deadline: November 1, with notification in June

The Colonial Players, Inc.
Theater-in-the-Round
108 East Street
Annapolis, MD 21401
(301) 956–3397

Program/Award: Biennial Promising Playwright Award
Description: Monetary award and showcase for script by aspiring playwright.
Restrictions: Limited to U.S. citizens or residents, or residents of U.S. possessions. Full-length plays suitable for arena production, running not less than 90 minutes excluding intermission. Maximum cast size 20; preference for cast of 12 or fewer. Plays submitted must be free of royalty and copyright restrictions that would prevent Colonial Players from producing them. Collaborations of 2 or more authors okay. If adaptations are used, source must be identified and manuscript must be accompanied by release form from holder of original copyright. Play must not have been formally produced elsewhere at time of submission. Staged readings and/or workshop productions are permitted.
Type of art: Playwriting
$ given: $750 plus consideration for production
Number of awards: 1 per year
Contact: Colonial Players, c/o Doris Cummins, Coordinator, 104 Stewart Drive, Edgewater, MD 21037
Application: Please write to request rules. Scripts must be typewritten and firmly bound. Author's name and address should not appear on manuscript, but be attached to manuscript in sealed envelope. $5 entry fee per play.
Deadline: Submissions accepted between September 1 and De-

cember 31 of even-numbered years, with notification by August of following odd-numbered years

Jacksonville University
Division of Art, Theatre Arts and Dance
2800 University Boulevard, North
Jacksonville, FL 32211
(904) 744–3950, ext. 3374

Program/Award: Annual Playwriting Contest
Description: Cash awards and premiere production of original, unproduced plays—full-length or one-act.
Restrictions: No restrictions on applicants. Scripts must be original, previously unproduced, full-length or one-act. Each playwright may submit up to 3 scripts.
Type of art: Playwriting
$ given: $1,000 minimum to help compensate for playwright's expenses for plays to be premiered
Number of awards: Varies; 2 awards for the year 1985–86, none for 1989 or 1990
Contact: Dr. Davis Sikes, Director, Annual Playwriting Contest
Application information: Write for annual rules and instructions.
Deadline: January 1; notification April 15

Jewish Community Center
3505 Mayfield Road
Cleveland Heights, OH 44118
(216) 382-4000

Program/Award: Jewish Community Center of Cleveland Playwriting Award Competition
Description: Cash prize and staged reading by Jewish Community Center Theatre, Cleveland, for a new play that provides fresh and significant perspectives on the range of Jewish experience.
Restrictions: All entries must be original, not previously produced, suitable for full-length production, and concerned with the Jewish experience.
Type of art: Playwriting

$ given: $500 on announcement of award, $500 on or about date of reading to help cover "in residence" expenses during brief production period

Number of awards: 1 award per year

Contact: Dorothy Silver, Director, JCC Theatre, (216) 382-4000, ext. 275

Application information: All submissions must be accompanied by a SASE to ensure return. Manuscript should be submitted to the address above.

Deadline: December 15, with notification on or about June 1

National Endowment for the Arts
Theater Program
1100 Pennsylvania Avenue, NW
Washington, DC 20506

Program/Award: Fellowships for Playwrights

Description: Fellowships to assist playwrights of exceptional talent to set aside time for writing, research, travel, or career advancement.

Restrictions: N/A

Type of art: Playwriting

$ given: Up to $17,500 per fellowship, plus $2,500 to defray costs of a residency at a professional theater of the playwright's choice. Use of residency funds will be restricted to travel and living expenses associated with residency at host theater. One-year awards made in amounts up to $20,000; a limited number of 2-year awards of $37,500.

Number of awards: N/A

Contact: Grants Office/Theater

Application information: Write for application guidelines, forms, and deadline information.

National Repertory Theatre Foundation
P.O. Box 71011
Los Angeles, CA 90071
(213) 629-3762

Program/Award: National Play Award

Description: Cash award to playwright and to professional theater for a paid Equity production.

Restrictions: Script must not be a musical, translation, or adaptation. It must not have won any major awards nor had a professional production.

Type of art: Playwriting

$ given: $7,500 cash award to playwright; $5,000 to a qualified professional theater to aid production of the winning script

Number of awards: 1 per year

Contact: Raul Espinoza, Script Coordinator

Application information: No entry forms required; however, a brief biography of the author and a history of the play must be submitted with the script. Scripts must be presented in a professional format: in covers, typed, and legibly photocopied. All entries will be prescreened by a staff of readers under the supervision of Lloyd Steele, NRTF Governor, writer, and drama critic. Each eligible entry will be read by at least 2 readers. Information may be obtained by writing and enclosing SASE.

Deadline: October 1, with notification during the fall

The Playwrights' Center
2301 Franklin Avenue East
Minneapolis, MN 55406
(612) 332-7481

Program/Award: McKnight Fellowships; Jerome Fellowships

Description: Fellowships to assist playwrights.

Restrictions: Eligibility criteria vary, depending on fellowship.

Type of art: Playwriting

$ given: McKnight Fellowship, $10,000 per grant for playwright to be in residence in Minneapolis for 2 months; Jerome Fellowship, $5,000 per grant for playwright to be in residence in Minneapolis for 1 year, with access to the Center's developmental services

Number of awards: 6 of each fellowship annually

Contact: Mike Coates, Office Manager

Application information: Write for details.

Deadline: Jerome Fellowship: February 1, with notification April 25; McKnight Fellowship: December 1

Forest A. Roberts Theatre
Northern Michigan University
Marquette, MI 49855-5364
(906) 227-2553

Program/Award: Forest A. Roberts/Shiras Institute Playwriting Award
Description: Cash award and university production of winning plays.
Restrictions: Vary from year to year.
Type of art: Playwriting
$ given: $1,000 plus fully mounted production and trip to Marquette to act as Artist-in-Residence during the 4-day run of the show. Conducting informal seminars and workshops will be a part of the residency.
Number of awards: 1 award per school year
Contact: Dr. James A. Panowski, Director
Application information: Write for brochure, which contains application information and entry blank.
Deadline: Varies; usually the Friday prior to Thanksgiving. Notification: Approx. April 15

Sunset Cultural Center
P.O. Box 5066
Carmel, CA 93921
(408) 624-3996

Program/Award: Festival of Firsts Playwriting Competition
Description: Competition to encourage and develop new plays for the theater.
Restrictions: Plays must be full-length and never produced before.
Type of art: Playwriting

$ given: $2,000 plus possible production
Number of awards: 1 annually
Contact: Richard Tyler, Director
Application information: Plays should be bound, with return envelopes included. Playwright must include a synopsis and character list of the play.
Deadline: August 31, with notification the following May

University of Chicago
Court Theatre
5706 South University
Chicago, IL 60637
(312) 702-7005

Program/Award: Charles H. Sergel Drama Prize
Description: Prizes offered biennially to encourage the writing of new American plays.
Restrictions: Only full-length original plays that have not been published or produced. Previous winners not eligible. Limited to U.S. citizens.
Type of art: Playwriting
$ given: $1,500 First Prize
Number of awards: 1 every other year
Contact: N/A
Application information: Contests in odd-numbered years. Information on contest available after January of odd years. No scripts accepted prior to January 1 of contest years. Entries must be accompanied by official entry blank.
Deadline: June 1

Wagner College
Department of Speech and Theatre
631 Howard Avenue
Staten Island, NY 10301
(212) 390-3256

Program/Award: Stanley Drama Award
Description: Annual award for best play or musical submitted to competition.

Restrictions: Script must not have been commercially produced or published; must be recommended by a theater professional.
Type of art: Playwriting
$ given: $1,000 per award
Number of awards: 1 annually
Contact: Bill Bly, Director, Stanley Drama Award
Application information: Script must be accompanied by completed application form and written recommendation.
Deadline: August 1, with notification in February/March

Also see: American Academy and Institute, Rodgers Award/COMPOSITION
Anisfield-Wolf Award in Race Relations/NONFICTION
Jenny McKean Moore Fund for Writers/FICTION
The Mary Roberts Rinehart Fund/NONFICTION
The San Francisco Foundation/FICTION

Other Theater

American College Theatre Festival
Kennedy Center for the Performing Arts
Washington, DC 20566
(202) 416-8000

Program/Award: American College Theatre Festival
Description: The American College Theatre Festival conducts 12 regional theater festivals with workshops for college and university students each year. As many as 20 of the most diverse regional college/university productions are invited to Washington, DC, to take part in a 2-week, noncompetitive national festival at the Kennedy Center, with all expenses paid. Several awards for playwriting are also available to Festival participants (see PLAYWRITING).
Restrictions: College and university theater organizations are eligible and encouraged to participate. Awards are given only to college and university students.
Type of art: Theater
$ given: Noncompetitive participation. Travel and expenses cov-

ered for festival participants. No cash awards for participation; awards for playwriting and musical composition listed elsewhere.

Number of awards: None

Contact: The Producing Director

Application information: Write for guidelines and application forms.

American College Theatre Festival
Kennedy Center for the Performing Arts
Washington, DC 20566
(202) 416-8000

Program/Award: Irene Ryan Acting Award

Description: Cash awards for outstanding college and university student actors.

Restrictions: Actors from college and university theater productions are eligible and encouraged to participate. Awards are given only to college and university students.

Type of art: Theater

$ given: 16 regional awards of $750 each, 2 top awards of $2,500 each, and a $500 award to the best acting partner of a regional finalist

Number of awards: 19

Contact: Kennedy Center, Irene Ryan Acting Award

Application information: Write for guidelines and application forms or apply through your college/university theater department.

Deadline: None

National Endowment for the Arts
Theater Program
1100 Pennsylvania Avenue, NW
Washington, DC 20506
(202) 682-5425

Program/Award: Director Fellowships

Description: Grants to individual stage directors of exceptional talent in their early career development. Opportunities may include working with one or more professional theaters, assisting and observing work of distinguished directors, or working on independent projects. This program is administered through Theatre Communications Group, (212) 697-5230.

Restrictions: N/A
Type of art: Theater
$ given: N/A
Number of awards: N/A
Contact: Grants Office/Theater, National Endowment for the Arts or Theatre Communications Group, (212) 697-5230
Application information: Write for information.

National Endowment for the Arts
Theater Program
1100 Pennsylvania Avenue, NW
Washington, DC 20506
(202) 682-5425

Program/Award: Distinguished Artist Fellowships in Theater
Description: Fellowships for artists in theater who are making extraordinary contributions to the art form. Four one-time fellowships awarded in recognition of an artist's overall contribution and record of accomplishment in the not-for-profit theater.
Restrictions: N/A
Type of art: Theater
$ given: N/A
Number of awards: 4 annually
Contact: Grants Office/Theater
Application information: Write for application guidelines and forms.

National Endowment for the Arts
Theater Program
1100 Pennsylvania Avenue, NW
Washington, DC 20506
(202) 682-5425

Program/Award: Stage Designer Fellowships

Description: Grants to encourage the development of early career stage designers in the not-for-profit theater.
Restrictions: N/A
Type of art: Theater
$ given: N/A
Number of awards: N/A
Contact: Grants Office/Theater
Application information: Write for application guidelines and forms.

Also see: Affiliate Artists Inc./PERFORMANCE—VOCAL

Creative Writing

Fiction

American Academy and Institute of Arts and Letters
633 West 155th Street
New York, NY 10032
(212) 368-5900

Program/Award: Academy-Institute Awards
Description: Annual awards to artists, composers, and writers who are not members of the Academy-Institute, to honor and encourage their creative work.
Restrictions: Limited to U.S. citizens or residents who are not members of the Academy-Institute.
Type of art: Composition, Creative Writing, Visual Art
$ given: $5,000 per award
Number of awards: 17 annually
Contact: Lydia Kaim, Assistant to Executive Director
Application information: No application may be submitted. By nomination from membership only. Recipients chosen by a committee of writers drawn from the membership and appointed by the Board.

American Academy and Institute of Arts and Letters
633 West 155th Street
New York, NY 10032
(212) 368-5900

Program/Award: The Sue Kaufman Prize for First Fiction; The Harold D. Vursell Memorial Award
Description: The Kaufman Prize is given annually for the best published work of first fiction (novel or collection of short stories) of the preceding year. The Vursell Award is given annually to single out recent writing in book form that merits recognition for the quality of its prose style.
Restrictions: Limited to U.S. citizens or residents.
Type of art: Fiction, Nonfiction
$ given: Kaufman Prize, $2,500; Vursell Award, $5,000
Number of awards: 1 of each annually
Contact: Lydia Kaim, Assistant to Executive Director
Application information: No application may be submitted. Recipients are chosen by a committee of writers drawn from the membership and appointed by the Board.

American Academy and Institute of Arts and Letters
633 West 155th Street
New York, NY 10032
(212) 368-5900

Program/Award: Rome Fellowship in Literature
Description: Annual residential fellowship in literature at the American Academy in Rome.
Restrictions: Limited to U.S. citizens.
Type of art: Creative Writing
$ given: $13,000 per award
Number of awards: 1 annually
Contact: Lydia Kaim, Assistant to Executive Director
Application information: No application may be submitted. Recipients chosen by a committee of writers drawn from the membership and appointed by the Board.

American Academy and Institute of Arts and Letters
633 West 155th Street
New York, NY 10032
(212) 368-5900

Program/Award: Richard and Hinda Rosenthal Foundation
   Awards
Description: Annual award for that American work of fiction
   published during the preceding 12 months which, though not
   a commercial success, is a considerable literary achievement.
   A second annual award to a younger American painter of
   distinction who has not yet been accorded due recognition.
Restrictions: Limited to U.S. citizens.
Type of art: Fiction, Painting
$ given: $5,000 per award
Number of awards: 1 annually in each category (2 total)
Contact: Lydia Kaim, Assistant to Executive Director
Application information: No application may be submitted. Re-
   cipient chosen by a committee of writers drawn from the
   membership and appointed by the Board.

American Academy and Institute of Arts and Letters
633 West 155th Street
New York, NY 10032
(212) 368-5900

Program/Award: The Mildred and Harold Strauss Livings
Description: Two awards that provide writers of English prose
   literature, other than plays, with an annual stipend to cover
   their living expenses so that they can devote their time exclusively to writing. Given for 5 years.
Restrictions: Candidates must be U.S. citizens or permanent residents.
Type of art: Fiction, Nonfiction
$ given: $50,000 a year for five years for each recipient
Number of awards: 2 awards concurrently
Contact: Lydia Kaim, Assistant to Executive Director
Application information: No application may be submitted. By
   nomination from membership only. Recipients chosen by a

committee of writers drawn from the membership and appointed by the Board.

Associated Writing Programs
c/o Old Dominion University
Norfolk, VA 23529-0079
(804) 683-3840

Program/Award: AWP Award Series in Short Fiction; AWP Award Series in Poetry; AWP Award Series in the Novel; AWP Award Series in Nonfiction
Description: Open competitions for book-length manuscripts: collection of short stories; collection of poems; a novel; or a work of nonfiction.
Restrictions: Limited to original works written in English.
Type of art: Poetry, Fiction, Nonfiction
$ given: Award winners: $1,000 cash honorarium per award plus publication by a university press; finalists: AWP acts as nonprofit agent, attempting to place their works with university, independent, and commercial publishers.
Number of awards: 1 winner per category; 3 finalists per category
Contact: D.W. Fenza, Publications Manager
Application information: Send SASE for guidelines before submitting. Submit typed, double-spaced manuscript in duplicate (one copy in the Novel Series), arranged as the author would prefer to see the book published, to the AWP in Norfolk, along with SASE for return of manuscript, and a $10 entry/reading fee.
Deadline: Manuscripts are accepted only during January and February

The John Dos Passos Prize for Literature
Department of English
Longwood College
Formville, VA 23901
(804) 392-9356

Program/Award: The John Dos Passos Prize for Literature

Description: Cash award and gold medal for literary achievement, to recognize excellence by American creative writers.
Restrictions: Writer must have substantial publication record and critical acclaim for work in fiction or nonfiction. Preference given to writers in mid-career whose work is experimental in nature, wide in scope, and/or consonant with the work of the author for whom the prize is named.
Type of art: Fiction, Nonfiction
$ given: $1,000 per award
Number of awards: 1 annually
Contact: Craig Challender, Chair, Dos Passos Prize Committee
Application information: By nomination only. Writers may not apply for consideration. Winner is chosen by independent jury.

Friends of American Writers
506 Rose Street
Des Plaines, IL 60016
(708) 827-8339

Program/Award: Annual Book Awards
Description: Four awards annually for published books with a Midwestern author or with a Midwestern locale: two cash awards for adult books, two cash awards for juvenile books.
Restrictions: Author must either be a current resident of one of 16 midwestern states, or have lived there for at least 5 years, or have set the work there. States include: Arkansas, Illinois, Indiana, Iowa, Kansas, Kentucky, Michigan, Minnesota, Missouri, Nebraska, North Dakota, Ohio, Oklahoma, South Dakota, Tennessee, and Wisconsin. The author shall not have published more than 3 books in the field and shall not have received a previous major monetary award of $1,000 or more. Books must have been published within the calendar year of the award.
Type of art: Fiction, Nonfiction
$ given: Adult category: $1,200 First Prize; $750 Second Prize. Juvenile category: $700 First Prize; $400 Second Prize
Number of awards: 4 awards annually
Contact: Vivian Mortensen, Awards Chairman

Application information: No application necessary. Send 2 copies of the book to the Awards Chairman.
Deadline: December 1, with notification in April

Great Lakes Colleges Association New Writer Awards
English Department
Albion College
Albion, MI 49224
(517) 629-1271

Program/Award: New Writer Awards
Description: Awards for yearly best book of fiction and best book of poetry.
Restrictions: Book must be first book by the author.
Type of art: Fiction, Poetry
$ given: Winners invited to tour up to 12 Great Lakes Colleges. Honorarium (at least $150 per college) and expenses paid.
Number of awards: 1 fiction award, 1 poetry award per year
Contact: Paul Loukides, Director, New Writer Awards
Application information: Only publishers may submit entries. Publishers may submit one book in each category, 4 copies of each book submitted. Send for rules, enclosing SASE.
Deadline: Usually February 28 deadline, with notification in May; write for current year deadline.

The Ingersoll Prizes
934 Main Street
Rockford, IL 61103
(815) 964-3242

Program/Award: The T. S. Eliot Award for Creative Writing; The Richard M. Weaver Award for Scholarly Letters
Description: Awards to honor authors of abiding importance and to call public attention to their works.
Restrictions: Limited to authors of international eminence in literature and humanities.
Type of art: Creative Writing, Humanities
$ given: $15,000 per award
Number of awards: 1 of each annually

Contact: Dr. John A. Howard, President

Application information: Awardees are chosen by the Executive Committee of The Ingersoll Prizes with the counsel of an annually selected panel of advisors. Applications and nominations are not accepted from other sources.

Jerusalem International Book Fair
212 Jaffa Road
P.O.B. 1241
Jerusalem 94383 Israel
02-382545, 380896; FAX: 972-2-385535

Program/Award: The Jerusalem Prize

Description: International literary prize given to honor an author who has contributed to the world's understanding of the "Freedom of the Individual in Society." The winner is a guest of the annual Jerusalem International Book Fair for its duration and receives a cash prize and a citation. The works of the prize winner are also exhibited at the Fair.

Restrictions: Jurors are not limited by the author's residence, race, or religion.

Type of art: Creative Writing

$ given: $5,000 cash prize plus citation

Number of awards: 1 per Fair

Contact: N/A

Application information: Write for information.

Note: Former recipients of the prize are Bertrand Russell, Max Frisch, André Schwartz-Bart, Ignazio Silone, Jorge Luis Borges, Eugene Ionesco, Simone de Beauvoir, Octavio Paz, Isaiah Berlin, Graham Greene, V. S. Naipaul, Milan Kundera, John M. Coetzee, and Ernesto Sabato.

Jenny McKean Moore Fund for Writers
3306 Highland Place, NW
Washington, DC 20008
(202) 363-8628

Program/Award: Visiting Lecturer in Creative Writing

Description: Grant sponsored jointly by the Fund and George

Washington University, for a writer to spend a year as visiting lecturer, teaching 2 courses per semester, one for university students and one for the community.

Restrictions: Open to any published writer with some teaching experience and sympathetic responses to student writers of all ages and social backgrounds.

Type of art: Creative Writing, Playwriting

$ given: Approx. $31,000 for one year

Number of awards: 1 lecturer position annually

Contact: Chris Sten, Chairman, Department of English, George Washington University, Washington, DC 20052

Application information: Application should be made by letter, listing publications, teaching experience, and other qualifications. Résumé, writing samples, a proposal for the university course, and 3 letters of recommendation addressing teaching abilities are required.

Deadline: November 15, with notification in late March for the following school year

The National Book Awards
155 Bank Street, Studio 1002-D
New York, NY 10014
(212) 206-0024

Program/Award: The National Book Awards

Description: The publishing industry's annual awards for literary excellence in fiction and general nonfiction.

Restrictions: Books must have been published in the U.S. by U.S. publishers and written by U.S. citizens.

Type of art: Fiction, Nonfiction

$ given: Winners in each category receive cash prizes of $10,000 each, plus Louise Nevelson wall sculpture; 5 runners-up in each category receive awards of $1,000 each.

Number of awards: 12 annually

Contact: Barbara Prete, Executive Director

Application information: Books must be nominated by their publishers. Entry fee of $100 per title. Send to address above for entry form with detailed requirements and regulations.

Deadline: July 31. Notification: Generally the 3rd week in November; a short list of nominations in each category is published in mid-October

National Endowment for the Arts
Literature Program
1100 Pennsylvania Avenue, NW
Washington, DC 20506
(202) 682-5451

Program/Award: Fellowships for Creative Writers; Fellowships for Translators
Description: Fellowships to published creative writers and translators of exceptional talent.
Restrictions: Limited to U.S. citizens or permanent residents.
Type of art: Fiction, Poetry, Nonfiction, Translation
$ given: $20,000 per Creative Writer fellowship; $10,000 to $20,000 per Translator fellowship, depending upon length and scope of project
Number of awards: N/A
Contact: Program Administrator, Literature Program
Application information: Application guidelines and forms available upon request.

The Paris Review
Editorial Office
541 East 72nd Street
New York, NY 10021
(212) 861-0016

Program/Award: Aga Khan Prize for Fiction
Description: Prize for best short story submitted to *The Paris Review* during the year.
Restrictions: Open to any story in English, between 1,000 and 10,000 words long.
Type of art: Fiction
$ given: $1,000 upon publication in *The Paris Review*
Number of awards: 1 annually

Contact: The Aga Khan Prize
Application information: Submit manuscript with SASE to above address.
Deadline: June 1

PEN American Center
568 Broadway
New York, NY 10012
(212) 334-1660

Program/Award: Ernest Hemingway Foundation Award
Description: Award for the first published book of fiction—either novel or short story collection—by an American writer, published during the current calendar year.
Restrictions: Book must be the first book published by the American writer, published in English during the current calendar year by an established publishing house. Genre fiction not eligible, nor are juvenile titles.
Type of art: Fiction
$ given: $7,500 per award
Number of awards: 1 annually
Contact: John Morrone, Program Coordinator
Application information: Submit 2 copies of eligible books to the Ernest Hemingway Foundation Award, in care of the above address.
Deadline: December 31 of the year in which book was published

PEN Syndicated Fiction
7815 Old Georgetown Road
Bethesda, MD 20814

Program/Award: PEN Syndicated Fiction Project
Description: Cash awards and publication of selected short stories in newspapers. Purpose of awards is to make quality fiction available to the general public and provide an outlet for writers' works.
Restrictions: Limited to short fiction (no longer than 2,500 words

per story), previously unpublished, or published in literary magazines with circulation of less than 2,000 copies. Anyone is eligible to submit.

Type of art: Fiction

$ given: $500 per winning story plus $100 each time the story is published by a newspaper

Number of awards: Varies; 60 awards for 1987

Contact: Caroline Marshall, Executive Director

Application information: Write for guidelines; do not submit without obtaining the submission guidelines first. Annual reading period is January 1–31.

Deadline: January 31

PEN/Faulkner Award for Fiction
Folger Shakespeare Library
201 East Capitol Street, SE
Washington, DC 20003
(202) 544-7077

Program/Award: PEN/Faulkner Award for Fiction

Description: Cash awards for a winning author and 4 nominees, to honor literary excellence.

Restrictions: Recipients must be American authors published within the calendar year of the award.

Type of art: Fiction

$ given: $7,500 for winner; $2,500 for each of 4 nominees

Number of awards: 5 annually

Contact: Janice Delaney, Executive Director

Application information: Candidates should submit 4 copies of their books before the end of the calendar year in which they were published.

Deadline: December 31, with notification by March 1

Redbook Magazine
224 West 57th Street
New York, NY 10019
(212) 649-3450

Program/Award: Redbook's Short Story Contest

Description: Open competition for short fiction; to reward the mastery of the short story form by writers whose fiction has not yet appeared in a major publication.

Restrictions: Write for complete rules (Redbook Magazine, Short Story Contest Rules) or see March issue of *Redbook* magazine for rules. Contestants must be over age 18 at time of entry; must not have had a story in a major publication; may submit only one short story no longer than 20 pages (5,000 words) by May 31; and must enclose a manuscript-sized SASE.

Type of art: Fiction

$ given: First Prize, $2,000 plus publication in *Redbook* magazine; Second Prize, $1,000; and Third Prize, $500

Number of awards: 3 prizes each year

Contact: Short Story Contest

Application information: Write for details.

Deadline: May 31, with notification by November 1

Note: Redbook reserves the right to purchase any story entered in the contest for up to 6 months after the contest deadline, at standard rates.

The San Francisco Foundation
685 Market Street
Suite 910
San Francisco, CA 94105
(415) 543-0223

Program/Award: Joseph Henry Jackson Award in Literature; James D. Phelan Award in Literature

Description: Awards to the authors of unpublished, partly completed book-length works of fiction, nonfiction, short stories, or poetry; the Phelan Award includes drama as well. Also, a special fund has been donated by Mary Tanenbaum in memory of J. H. Jackson to encourage the writing of nonfiction. From this fund, an award may be made for a manuscript of nonfiction submitted in either the Jackson or Phelan competitions, but not selected to receive either of those awards.

Restrictions: The Jackson Award is limited to individuals who have been residents of northern California or Nevada for the 3 consecutive years immediately prior to January 15 of the year of application. The Phelan Award is limited to individuals born in California. For both awards, applicants must be age 20–35 as of January 15 of the year of application. Their writing need not concern California. Applicants may compete for both awards and in more than one type of literature, but may win only one award. A single manuscript and application form can serve for both awards (if the applicant is eligible for both).

Type of art: Fiction, Nonfiction, Poetry, Drama
$ given: $2,000 each for Jackson and Phelan awards; $1,000 for special fund award, if given
Number of awards: Maximum of 3 awards annually
Contact: Awards Office
Application information: Write for official application forms after November 1.
Deadline: January 15, with notification by June 15

Southwest Review
6410 Airline Road
Southern Methodist University
Dallas, TX 75275
(214) 373-7440

Program/Award: John H. McGinnis Memorial Award
Description: Award to encourage and reward literary excellence; made in alternate years for fiction and nonfiction.
Restrictions: All fiction and nonfiction pieces published in the *Southwest Review* are considered eligible.
Type of art: Fiction, Nonfiction
$ given: $1,000 per award
Number of awards: 1 annually
Contact: Willard Spiegelman, Editor
Application information: No separate application, other than submission for publication in *Southwest Review*.
Deadline: None. Notification: Announcement of winner in winter issue of magazine

Stanford University
Department of English
Stanford, CA 94305

Program/Award: Wallace E. Stegner Fellowships in Creative Writing
Description: International, competitive fellowships for talented young writers with proposed or in-progress projects.
Restrictions: N/A
Type of art: Fiction, Poetry
$ given: $4,500 for 1-year residence/instruction/criticism at the Stanford University Creative Writing Center. Fellows enroll in and pay tuition for advanced fiction or poetry writing seminars; they may be admitted as regular undergraduate or graduate students.
Number of awards: 4 fellowships in fiction; 2 fellowships in poetry, annually
Contact: N/A
Application information: Application requires project prospectus or outline, 2 sample chapters (50 pages), 2–3 short stories, or 12 poems.
Deadline: January 15, with notification June 1 for following school year

University of Edinburgh
Department of English Literature
David Hume Tower, George Square
Edinburgh EH8 9JX, Scotland
031-667 1011

Program/Award: James Tait Black Memorial Prizes
Description: Prizes given for the best work of fiction and the best biography published in the previous calendar year, in the opinion of the Professor of English Literature at the University.
Restrictions: Works must be fiction and biography, written in English, originating with a British publisher, and first published in Britain in the year of the award. (Technical publica-

tion elsewhere, simultaneously or even a little earlier, does not disqualify.) The nationality of the writer is irrelevant. Both prizes may go to the same author, but neither to the same author a second time.

Type of art: Fiction, Biography

$ given: £1,500 per prize

Number of awards: 2 prizes annually, one for fiction and one for biography

Contact: James Tait Black Prize

Application information: Only publishers may submit works for consideration; individual authors may not apply. Publishers are invited to submit a copy of any work of fiction or biography that, in their judgment, may merit consideration for the award.

Deadline: None, with notification usually in February

The University of Iowa
Writers' Workshop—436 EPB
Iowa City, IA 52242
(319) 335-0416

Program/Award: Iowa Short Fiction Award; John Simmons Short Fiction Award

Description: Cash awards plus publication for short story collections.

Restrictions: Entry must be a collection of short stories, totaling at least 150 typed pages. Stories previously published in periodicals are eligible for inclusion. Any writer who has not previously published a volume of prose fiction is eligible to enter.

Type of art: Fiction

$ given: $1,000 for each award, plus publication of the collection by the University of Iowa Press

Number of awards: 2 annually

Contact: N/A

Application information: No application forms are necessary. Submit manuscript with SASE of appropriate size for return.

Deadline: Submissions accepted between August 1 and September 30

University of New Mexico
Department of English
Albuquerque, NM 87131
(505) 277-6347

Program/Award: D. H. Lawrence Fellowship
Description: Fellowship for creative writers, providing cash prize and summer residency at Lawrence ranch near Taos, New Mexico.
Restrictions: N/A
Type of art: Creative Writing
$ given: $2,100 cash prize plus 8–10 weeks' summer lodging at Lawrence ranch
Number of awards: 1 annually
Contact: D. H. Lawrence Fellowship
Application information: Write for application forms and guidelines. A $15 processing fee must accompany formal application.
Deadline: End of January

Virginia Quarterly Review
One West Range
Charlottesville, VA 22903
(804) 924-3124

Program/Award: Emily Clark Balch Awards
Description: Cash awards for best published short story and best published poem.
Restrictions: N/A
Type of art: Fiction, Poetry
$ given: $500 for each award
Number of awards: 2 annually
Contact: Staige D. Blackford, Editor
Application: Write for further information.

Also see: American Academy and Institute, Jean Stein Award/
  NONFICTION
  American Academy and Institute, Zabel Award/PO-
  ETRY

American Academy in Rome/ARCHITECTURE
Anisfield-Wolf Award in Race Relations/NONFIC-
TION
The Boston Globe, Winship Book Award/NONFIC-
TION
Carnegie Fund for Authors/NONFICTION
Coordinating Council of Literary Magazines/POETRY
Fine Arts Work Center in Provincetown/SCULPTURE
The Friends of Literature, Shakespeare Awards/NON-
FICTION
Institute of International Education, Cintas/PRINT-
MAKING
JWB Jewish Book Council/NONFICTION
PEN American Center, Revson Fellowships/POETRY
The Mary Roberts Rinehart Fund/NONFICTION

Nonfiction

American Academy and Institute of Arts and Letters
633 West 155th Street
New York, NY 10032
(212) 368-5900

Program/Award: The Jean Stein Award
Description: Annual award given in successive years to a writer
of fiction, nonfiction, and poetry whose work takes risks
in expressing its commitment to the author's values and vision.
Restrictions: Limited to U.S. citizens and residents.
Type of art: Fiction, Nonfiction, Poetry
$ given: $5,000 per award
Number of awards: 1 annually
Contact: Lydia Kaim, Assistant to Executive Director
Application information: No application may be submitted. Recipients chosen by a committee of writers drawn from the
membership and appointed by the Board.

American Society of Composers, Authors and Publishers (ASCAP)
One Lincoln Plaza, 6th Floor
New York, NY 10023
(212) 595-3050

Program/Award: ASCAP—Deems Taylor Awards
Description: Awards for the best nonfiction books and for the best articles about music and/or its creators.
Restrictions: Open to any works published anywhere in the U.S. in English during the calendar year preceding the award.
Type of art: Nonfiction
$ given: $500 per book award; $250 per article award
Number of awards: Varies from year to year, depending upon judges' determination.
Contact: Michael A. Kerker
Application information: Write to the address above.
Deadline: April 30

Anisfield-Wolf Award in Race Relations
321 Cherry Hill Road
Princeton, NJ 08540
(609) 924-3756

Program/Award: Anisfield-Wolf Awards in Race Relations
Description: Annual awards for published scholarly books in the field of race relations and for published works of creative literature concerned with racial problems.
Restrictions: Open to published works (no works-in-progress) in any field which in any way contribute to the betterment of race relations or a clearer understanding of the mechanisms or injustices of racism.
Type of art: Fiction, Nonfiction, Poetry
$ given: $3,000 stipend per book
Number of awards: 2 awards per year, one for scholarly work and one for a work of creative literature (fiction, poetry, biography, autobiography, drama)
Contact: Ashley Montagu, Chairman
Application information: Send a copy of the book in published

form to each of the 3 following judges: (1) Ashley Montagu, 321 Cherry Hill Road, Princeton, NJ 08540; (2) Gwendolyn Brooks, 7428 South Evans Avenue, Chicago IL 60619; (3) Oscar Handlin, Widener Library, Harvard University, Cambridge MA 02138.

Deadline: January 31, with notification in March/April

Arts Management Pty. Limited
56 Kellett Street
Potts Point, NSW 2011, Australia
(02) 356 2400; FAX (02) 358 4417

Program/Award: Miles Franklin Award
Description: Annual cash award for a published book on Australian life.
Restrictions: No specific requirements as regards nationality, age, etc., but the book must be first published in the year entered and "must depict Australian life in any of its phases."
Type of art: Creative Writing
$ given: $10,000 (Australian) per award
Number of awards: 1 annually
Contact: Kate Gralton, Assistant
Application information: More than 1 entry may be submitted per applicant. The Permanent Trustee Company Limited must be notified of the title of the proposed entry within 28 days following publication. Copies of proposed entries are to be submitted by the author (or by the publisher with the author's authority). Where entries have been published in December, they must be submitted by January 31; in all other cases, they should be submitted within 2 months of publication. Send one copy directly to each judge and one copy to Permanent Trustee Company Limited. All packages containing entries should be clearly marked "Miles Franklin Literary Award Entry." Write for complete application information and the addresses of the judges.
Deadline: January 31, with notification in May/June

The Boston Globe
135 Morrissey Boulevard
Boston, MA 02107
(617) 929-2649

Program/Award: Laurence L. Winship Book Award
Description: Cash prize to the author of the best book published
   between July 1 of previous year and June 30 of award year,
   having some relation to New England—author, theme, plot,
   or locale.
Restrictions: Excluded—children's books, poetry, anthologies.
Type of art: Fiction, Nonfiction
$ given: $2,000 per award
Number of awards: 1 annually
Contact: N/A
Application information: Books must be submitted by publisher
   rather than by author. Judges request that books be submitted
   as published, to allow for careful examination by full panel.
   Six copies of each book nominated should be sent to the
   address above.
Deadline: June 30. Notification: At the annual Boston Globe
   Book Award in the fall

Carnegie Fund for Authors
330 Sunrise Highway
Rockville Centre, NY 11570

Description: Grants-in-aid for authors who are in need, i.e., who
   have suffered a financial emergency as the result of illness or
   injury to the author, spouse, or dependent child, or who have
   suffered some equivalent misfortune.
Restrictions: Limited to authors who have published (commercially) at least one book of reasonable length that has received
   reader acceptance. "Vanity" books not acceptable.
Type of art: Fiction, Nonfiction, Poetry
$ given: Grants vary according to needs of applicant
Number of awards: N/A
Contact: William L. Rothenberg, Trustee

Application information: Application forms may be requested in writing.
Deadline: None

The Friends of Literature
c/o Mrs. Mabel A. Munger, President
300 North State Street, Apt. 4227
Chicago, IL 60610
(312) 321-1459

Program/Award: Annual Shakespeare Birthday Dinner and Awards Program
Description: Awards for best fiction, nonfiction, poetry, and civic contribution to Chicago-based writers.
Restrictions: Author must have had a connection with Chicago or the Chicago metropolitan area at some time during his or her life and/or career. Books must be published by a recognized trade publisher. Works must be of literary or scholarly merit; manuals, guides, reference works, and cookbooks are not eligible.
Type of art: Fiction, Nonfiction, Poetry
$ given: $500 fiction award; $500 nonfiction award; $300 fiction/nonfiction award; $250 fiction/nonfiction award; $200 poetry award
Number of awards: 6 awards total in 1984
Contact: Mrs. Mabel A. Munger, President
Application information: Submit 2 copies of book for review.
Deadline: January 15, with notification first Saturday in May

JWB Jewish Book Council
15 East 26th Street
New York, NY 10010
(212) 532-4949

Program/Award: National Jewish Book Awards
Description: Awards in 11 categories to promote greater awareness of works of Jewish literature and scholarship. Categories:

Jewish History; Israel; Jewish Thought; Fiction; Holocaust; Children's Literature; Yiddish Literature; Visual Arts; Scholarship; Illustrated Children's Book; Biography.

Restrictions: Books must be on Jewish subjects and themes. Books must be published during the preceding calendar year. No anthologies of previously published material, collections of writings by various authors, or reprints and revised editions. No manuscripts. Books must be published in the English language unless otherwise specified. This includes books translated into English from any other language. The author/translator must be a resident or citizen of the U.S. or Canada.

Type of art: Fiction, Nonfiction, Poetry (Yiddish only)

$ given: $750 per award

Number of awards: 11 annually, one in each category

Contact: Paula G. Gottlieb, Director

Application information: Write for details. Submission must be made by publisher.

PEN American Center
568 Broadway
New York, NY 10012
(212) 334-1660

Program/Award: PEN/Martha Albrand Award for Nonfiction; PEN/Martha Albrand Award for Poetry

Description: Prizes given for a first-published book of general nonfiction distinguished by qualities of literary and stylistic excellence; and for a debut book of verse.

Restrictions: Eligible books must have been published in the calendar year under consideration. Authors must be U.S. citizens or permanent residents. Although there are no restrictions upon the subject of titles submitted for the nonfiction award, books such as how-to guides, cookery and craft manuals, or celebrity fan books will not be considered. Books should be adult nonfiction for the general or academic reader.

Type of art: Nonfiction, Poetry

$ given: $1,000 per award

Number of awards: 1 of each annually
Contact: N/A
Application information: Publishers, authors, or agents may
   submit 3 copies of each eligible book to the address above.
Deadline: December 31

PEN American Center
568 Broadway
New York, NY 10012
(212) 334-1660

Program/Award: PEN/Jerard Fund Award
Description: Prize given to a woman writer at an early point in
   her career to honor a work-in-progress of general nonfiction
   distinguished by high literary quality.
Restrictions: The minimum requirement for application is the
   publication of at least one magazine article in a national publication or in a major literary magazine. Applicants must not
   have published more than 1 book of any kind. Although there
   are no restrictions upon the content of the work, the emphasis
   is on the quality of writing rather than the subject. Purely
   topical or journalistic subjects are discouraged. Manuscripts
   such as how-to manuals, cookery or craft books, and fashion
   guides are not considered. Work-in-progress must be an En-
   glish-language, book-length work of nonfiction. Applicants
   must be U.S. residents. No age restrictions.
Type of art: Nonfiction
$ given: $3,000 per award
Number of awards: 1 annually
Contact: John Morrone, Programs Coordinator
Application information: Each applicant should submit 2 copies
   of no more than 50 pages of her book-length nonfiction work-
   in-progress, accompanied by a list of her publications. Manuscripts are judged by a panel of 5 American nonfiction writers,
   3 of whom are women. Manuscripts returned only if appropriate SASE accompanies submission.
Deadline: February 15

The Mary Roberts Rinehart Fund
Department of English
George Mason University
4400 University Drive
Fairfax, VA 22030
(703) 323-2936

Program/Award: Grants in Aid

Description: Two grants made annually to writers who need financial assistance not otherwise available to complete work showing promise. Grants given in 2 of 4 categories—fiction/poetry and drama/nonfiction—on an alternate basis. Fiction/poetry in even-numbered years; drama/nonfiction in odd-numbered years. Preference shown to new or relatively unknown writers.

Restrictions: By nomination only to unpublished creative writers who need financial assistance to complete works of fiction, poetry, drama, biography, autobiography, or history with a strong narrative quality. Although most nominations come from writing program faculty around the country, any unpublished writer is eligible to be nominated by a sponsoring writer or editor. Unpublished is defined as having no book publication.

Type of art: Creative Writing, Playwriting

$ given: Varies with Fund income; currently approx. $950 per award

Number of awards: 2 annually

Contact: Roger Lathbury, Director

Application information: Nomination by established writers or editors. The Fund will consider the submission of a candidate's work by any established writer or editor as nomination for a grant; no written recommendations are necessary. Work submitted must be a manuscript in English, up to 30 pages for fiction, nonfiction, and drama; up to 25 pages for poetry.

Deadline: November 30, with notification March 1

Syracuse University Press
1600 Jamesville Avenue
Syracuse, NY 13244-5160
(315) 443-5534

Program/Award: John Ben Snow Prize
Description: Competition to encourage the writing of books of
genuine significance and literary distinction that will augment
knowledge of New York State. Cash grant and publication of
winning manuscript by Syracuse University Press.
Restrictions: Work must be nonfiction, dealing with the physical,
historical, and/or cultural characteristics of New York State.
Manuscript must be previously unpublished and not under
consideration by another publisher or for another award. Fiction, poetry, juvenile books, and unrevised theses and disser-
tations not eligible. Manuscripts based on direct, personal
experience receive the same consideration as those relying on
scholarly research.
Type of art: Nonfiction
$ given: $1,500 prize plus publication by Syracuse University
Press. In the event of a tie, award is divided. Award may be
withheld for the year.
Number of awards: 1 annually (unless award is tied or withheld)
Contact: Director, John Ben Snow Prize
Application information: Applicants should write a letter of in-
quiry briefly describing the subject, scope, significance, and
length of their manuscripts.
Deadline: December 31, with notification in the spring

Verbatim, The Language Quarterly
4 Laurel Heights
Old Lyme, CT 06371
(203) 434-2104

Program/Award: Verbatim Essay Competition
Description: Cash awards to encourage good writing about language.
Restrictions: Limited to original popular articles, in English, not
exceeding 2,000 words. Articles will be judged on basis of

originality of presentation, accuracy, interest, and quality of writing.

Type of art: Nonfiction

$ given: $1,000 First Prize; $500 Second Prize; $250 each for Third through Sixth Prizes—plus publication for all in *Verbatim*

Number of awards: 6 annually

Contact: Verbatim Essay Competition

Application information: Send SASE for particulars. Entries must be submitted in typescript or clearly legible printout, on 8½-by-11-inch plain white paper with wide margins. Name of author must not appear anywhere in typescript, but should be typewritten on a 3-by-5-inch card clipped to the submission.

Deadline: October 31, with notification January 31

Also see: American Academy and Institute, Rome Fellowship/ FICTION

American Academy and Institute, Strauss Livings/FIC- TION

American Academy and Institute, Vursell Award/FIC- TION

American Academy and Institute, Zabel Award/PO- ETRY

American Academy in Rome/ARCHITECTURE

Associated Writing Programs/FICTION

Coordinating Council of Literary Magazines/POETRY

The John Dos Passos Prize for Literature/FICTION

Fine Arts Work Center in Provincetown/SCULPTURE

Friends of American Writers, Annual Book Awards/ FICTION

The Ingersoll Prizes/FICTION

Institute of International Education, Cintas/PRINT- MAKING

Jerusalem International Book Fair/FICTION

The National Book Awards/FICTION

National Endowment for the Arts, Fellowships/FIC- TION

The San Francisco Foundation/FICTION

Southwest Review/FICTION

University of Edinburgh/FICTION
University of New Mexico/FICTION

Poetry

The Academy of American Poets
177 East 87th Street
New York, NY 10128
(212) 427-5665

Program/Award: American Poets Fund
Description: Grants to assist poets of demonstrated ability who
   are in a state of financial need of an immediate and urgent
   nature. Grants from this fund may not be used to promote or
   otherwise to improve or enhance the literary talent or reputa-
   tion of the recipient, but are intended solely to relieve the
   recipient of burdens of financial distress.
Restrictions: Limited to U.S. citizens.
Type of art: Poetry
$ given: Varies, according to individual needs
Number of awards: N/A
Contact: N/A
Application information: Applications are not accepted; Academy Chancellors, Fellows, and prizewinners may bring the
   circumstances of qualifying poets to the attention of the
   American Poets Fund committee by sending a letter of nomination to the Executive Director of the Academy, including
   specific data concerning the nominee's current financial situation.

The Academy of American Poets
177 East 87th Street
New York, NY 10128
(212) 427-5665

Program/Award: Academy of American Poets Fellowship
Description: Fellowship awarded for distinguished poetic achieve-
   ment.
Restrictions: Winners must be living citizens of the U.S.

Type of art: Poetry
$ given: $10,000 per fellowship
Number of awards: 2 annually
Contact: Alex Thorburn, Program Director
Application information: Nomination by Academy Chancellors only. Interested persons may contact the Academy for further information.

The Academy of American Poets
177 East 87th Street
New York, NY 10128
(212) 427-5665

Program/Award: The Lamont Poetry Selection
Description: Award for a manuscript of original poetry in English by a living American poet who has published one book of poetry in other than a small edition. Suggested length is between 40–75 pages, but greater length will not disqualify.
Restrictions: Manuscript must be under contract and scheduled for publication. Poet must be living U.S. citizen.
Type of art: Poetry
$ given: $1,000 cash award directly to poet, plus Academy commitment to purchase 2,000 copies of the poet's book from the publisher
Number of awards: 1 annually
Contact: Alex Thorburn, Program Director
Application information: Only publishers may submit manuscripts for consideration. Write for guidelines and entry form. An official application form, together with 3 copies of the manuscript, must be submitted by the publisher to the address above.
Deadline: May 15

The Academy of American Poets
177 East 87th Street
New York, NY 10128
(212) 427-5665

Program/Award: The Harold Morton Landon Translation Award

Description: An annual award to an American poet for a published translation of poetry from any language into English. The translation may be a book-length poem, a collection of poems, or a verse drama translated into verse.

Restrictions: No anthologies or collaborations. Limited to U.S. citizens.

Type of art: Poetry

$ given: $1,000 per award

Number of awards: 1 annually

Contact: Alex Thorburn, Program Director

Application information: Publishers may submit published books to the address above.

Deadline: January 1

The Academy of American Poets
177 East 87th Street
New York, NY 10128
(212) 427-5665

Program/Award: Peter I. B. Lavan Younger Poets Award

Description: Award to a younger, published American poet.

Restrictions: Limited to U.S. citizens under age 40 who have published at least one full-length collection of poetry.

Type of art: Poetry

$ given: $1,000 per award

Number of awards: 3 annually

Contact: N/A

Application information: No applications accepted; nomination by Academy Chancellors only.

The Academy of American Poets
177 East 87th Street
New York, NY 10128
(212) 427-5665

Program/Award: The Walt Whitman Award

Description: Award to unpublished American poets.

Restrictions: Submitted manuscript (50–100 pages) must be of original poetry in English by a living poet who is a citizen of the U.S. and who has never had a book of poems more than 40 pages in length published in an edition of more than 500 copies.

Type of art: Poetry
$ given: $1,000; publication of manuscript; and Academy distribution of 1,500 copies to members and friends
Number of awards: 1 annually
Contact: N/A
Application information: An entry form, obtainable from the Academy, must accompany each manuscript. Send SASE to Academy for contest brochure and entry form. Send for guidelines and application form in late August only.
Deadline: Manuscripts are accepted between September 15 and November 15

American Academy and Institute of Arts and Letters
633 West 155th Street
New York, NY 10032
(212) 368-5900

Program/Award: The Morton Dauwen Zabel Award
Description: Award given each year to an American poet, writer of fiction, or critic, in rotation; the recipients are writers of progressive, original, and experimental tendencies rather than of academic and conservative tendencies.
Restrictions: Limited to U.S. citizens.
Type of art: Poetry, Fiction, Nonfiction
$ given: $2,500 per award
Number of awards: 1 annually
Contact: Lydia Kaim, Assistant to Executive Director
Application information: No applications may be submitted. By nomination from the membership only.

American Academy and Institute of Arts and Letters
633 West 155th Street
New York, NY 10032
(212) 368-5900

Program/Award: Witter Bynner Prize for Poetry

Description: Prize given annually to an outstanding younger poet.
Restrictions: N/A
Type of art: Poetry
$ given: $1,500 per award
Number of awards: 1 annually
Contact: Lydia Kaim, Assistant to Executive Director
Application information: No applications may be submitted. By nomination from the membership only.

Coordinating Council of Literary Magazines
666 Broadway
New York, NY 10012
(212) 614-6551

Program/Award: General Electric Foundation Awards for Younger Writers
Description: Annual cash awards to recognize 6 authors of poetry, fiction, or literary essays and the literary magazines that published their work.
Restrictions: Only CCLM member magazines may nominate writers whom they have published.
Type of art: Poetry, Fiction, Nonfiction
$ given: $5,000 per writer award; $1,000 per magazine
Number of awards: 6 awards annually to writers; 6 awards annually to magazines
Contact: Grants Program Director
Application information: Further information may be requested from the Grants Program Director in writing.

The Paris Review
Editorial Office
541 East 72nd Street
New York, NY 10021
(212) 861-0016

Program/Award: The Bernard F. Conners Poetry Prize

Description: Prize for best long poem (over 300 lines).
Restrictions: Open to any poem over 300 lines in English. Translations accepted if accompanied by original language version.
Type of art: Poetry
$ given: $1,000 per award upon publication in *The Paris Review*
Number of awards: 1 annually
Contact: Editorial Office
Application information: Submit manuscript with SASE between April 1 and May 1 only.
Deadline: May 1

PEN American Center
568 Broadway
New York, NY 10012
(212) 334-1660

Program/Award: PEN/Revson Foundation Fellowships
Description: Awards given in alternate years to a poet (odd-numbered years) and a writer of fiction (even-numbered years) under the age of 35. The fellowship is awarded on the basis of work-in-progress as well as the quality of work already published. The fellowship is designed to provide the writer with the financial sustenance required to devote an extended period of time to complete a book-length work-in-progress.
Restrictions: Candidate should be a writer in "early–mid career" whose body of work to date (normally no more than 2 books) has been marked by singular talent but has not been sufficiently recognized by the literary community and the reading public.
Type of art: Fiction, Poetry
$ given: $12,500 per fellowship
Number of awards: 1 annually, alternating between poetry and fiction
Contact: John Morrone
Application information: Candidates must be nominated by an editor or fellow writer. It is strongly recommended that the

nominator write a letter of support describing the literary quality of the candidate's work and explaining why the work has not yet met with the recognition it merits. Nominator needs to provide list of candidate's published work and samples of current work-in-progress. Three copies of no more than 50 pages of the current work, intended as part of a new book, must be submitted along with a suitable SASE for return.

Deadline: Fiction, February 15 of even years; notification in May. Poetry, September 1 of odd years; notification in December

Pitt Poetry Series
University of Pittsburgh Press
127 North Bellefield Avenue
Pittsburgh, PA 15260
(412) 624-4141

Program/Award: Agnes Lynch Starrett Poetry Prize
Description: Cash prize plus publication in the Pitt Poetry Series for winner of this competition.
Restrictions: Limited to manuscripts in English by writers who have not previously published a full-length book of poetry (defined as volume of 48 or more pages published in an edition of 750 or more copies; books whose publishing costs were borne by their authors are not excluded by this definition).
Type of art: Poetry
$ given: $2,000 plus book publication
Number of awards: 1 annually
Contact: Ed Ochester, Editor
Application information: Contestants must request and read a copy of the current rules before submitting manuscripts. Send SASE to Starrett Prize at address above. A $10 reading fee is required for each manuscript submitted. Competition is severe (850 applications in one recent year). Casual submissions are not encouraged. Publisher cannot provide critiques of manuscripts.
Deadline: Submissions accepted between March 1 and April 30 only. Notification: late summer

The Poetry Society
National Poetry Centre
21 Earls Court Square
London SW5 9DE, England
071-373 7861

Program/Award: The Alice Hunt Bartlett Award
Description: Prize awarded annually to the poet the Society most wishes to honor and encourage, for poems in a book published in English.
Restrictions: Poets of any nationality eligible. Special consideration to younger or newly emerged poets and to first published collections of their work. In such collections, there should be not fewer than 20 poems or 400 lines. For poems translated into English, the original poet must be alive and the prize will be divided equally between the poet and the translator.
Type of art: Poetry
$ given: £500 per award
Number of awards: 1 annually
Contact: Ms. Barbara Hill
Application information: The Society invites submissions from writers, publishers, and others. Three copies of any publication for consideration should be submitted to the Society's library in the year of publication.
Deadline: February 28

The Poetry Society of America
15 Gramercy Park
New York, NY 10003
(212) 254-9628

Description: Competitive poetry prizes; no grants or fellowships.
Restrictions: 10 awards open to the public and 9 awards open only to members of the Society.
Type of art: Poetry
$ given: Prizes vary in amount; total of $11,000 in annual support
Number of awards: Approx. 19 awards annually
Contact: Suzanne Wise, Assistant Director

Application information: Interested parties should send SASE after September 1 for details.

Quarterly Review of Literature
26 Haslet Avenue
Princeton, NJ 08540
(609) 452-4703

Program/Award: QRL Poetry Series
Description: Open competition for cash awards and publication in QRL Poetry Series.
Restrictions: Manuscripts containing a group of poems, a poetic play, or a group of translations should be 60–100 pages; single long poems of more than 30 pages are also eligible. Manuscript must be in English or translated into English; may be submitted from outside the U.S.
Type of art: Poetry
$ given: $1,000 to $5,000 per award
Number of awards: 4–6 in 1991
Contact: Renee Weiss, Editor
Application information: Send SASE for complete information on submitting manuscript. Only 1 manuscript per author may be entered per reading period. Each manuscript submitted must be accompanied by a subscription to the QRL Poetry Series (2 volumes for $20).
Deadline: Submissions may be made during May and October only; winners informed immediately

Delmore Schwartz Memorial Poetry Award Committee
c/o Professor M. L. Rosenthal
Department of English
New York University
19 University Place, Room 200
New York, NY 10003
(212) 998-8835

Program/Award: Delmore Schwartz Memorial Poetry Award
Description: Award occasionally conferred on outstanding poet by New York University through a committee of judges.

Restrictions: Candidate must be a younger poet who has published no more than one book, or an insufficiently recognized mature poet.

Type of art: Poetry

$ given: Average award, $1,000

Number of awards: 1 award, at intervals of one year or longer

Contact: Professor M. L. Rosenthal, Chairman

Application information: Applications and inquiries are not invited. Decisions are made by the committee of judges, made up of two poets.

Southwest Review
6410 Airline Road
Southern Methodist University
Dallas, TX 75275
(214) 373-7440

Program/Award: Elizabeth Matchett Stover Memorial Award

Description: Annual award in poetry.

Restrictions: Only poems published in *Southwest Review* during the year are eligible.

Type of art: Poetry

$ given: $100 per award

Number of awards: 1 annually

Contact: Willard Spiegelman, Editor

Application information: No separate application other than submission for publication in *Southwest Review.*

Deadline: None. Notification: Announcement in winter issue

The University of Massachusetts Press
P.O. Box 429
Amherst, MA 01004
(413) 545-2217

Program/Award: The Juniper Prize

Description: Monetary prize and publication of a book of poetry.

Restrictions: Requirements vary year by year. Generally, submissions must not exceed 60 pages in typescript (usually 50–60 poems). A list of poems published in literary journals and/or anthologies must accompany the manuscript. Such poems may be included in manuscript and must be identified. Manuscripts by more than one author, entries of more than one manuscript simultaneously or within the same year, and translations are not eligible. Manuscripts by University of Massachusetts employees and students, as well as manuscripts by previous winners of the Juniper Prize, are not eligible.

Type of art: Poetry

$ given: $1,000 prize (in lieu of royalties on the first print run) and publication by the Press. In the event of a tie, 2 awards of $500 may be granted and both manuscripts published.

Number of awards: 1 annually

Contact: Juniper Prize

Application information: Mail entries, with $10 submission fee and SASE of appropriate size for return, to: Juniper Prize, University of Massachusetts Press, c/o Mail Office, University of Massachusetts, Amherst, MA 01003.

Deadline: September 1, with notification in April/May and publication the following fall

University of Missouri Press
200 Lewis Hall
Columbia, MO 65211
(314) 882-7641

Program/Award: Breakthrough Books Series—Devins Award

Description: Cash award against royalties for best poetry book in the biennial contest, published by the University of Missouri Press in its Breakthrough Series.

Restrictions: Open to writers who have previously published in other media but whose works have not yet appeared in book form. Established writers who are using a particular creative form for the first time are also eligible.

Type of art: Poetry

$ given: $500 against royalties

Number of awards: 1 biennially

Contact: Breakthrough Editor

Application information: Send SASE for rules and entry blank.

Deadline: Submissions accepted between February 1 and March 30 of odd-numbered years

Yale University Library
Yale University
New Haven, CT 06520
(203) 432-1818

Program/Award: Bollingen Prize in Poetry
Description: Prizes given in odd-numbered years to American poet whose work is considered the highest achievement in the field of American poetry for the 2-year review period.
Restrictions: Open to any American poet whose work has been published during the review period and who has not previously won the Prize. Prior achievement is taken into consideration.
Type of art: Poetry
$ given: $10,000 per award
Number of awards: 1 every 2 years
Contact: Ralph W. Franklin, Beinecke Rare Book and Manuscript Library, Yale University, New Haven, CT 06520
Application information: Since the committee considers all eligible books automatically, authors and publishers are not encouraged to submit books.

Also see: American Academy and Institute, Rome Fellowship/ FICTION
American Academy and Institute, Jean Stein Award/ NONFICTION
American Academy in Rome/ARCHITECTURE
Anisfield-Wolf Award in Race Relations/NONFICTION
Associated Writing Programs/FICTION
Carnegie Fund for Authors/NONFICTION
Fine Arts Work Center in Provincetown/SCULPTURE
The Friends of Literature, Shakespeare Award/NONFICTION
Great Lakes Colleges Association/FICTION
The Ingersoll Prizes/FICTION

Institute of International Education, Cintas/PRINT-
MAKING
JWB Jewish Book Council/NONFICTION
Jenny McKean Moore Fund for Writers/FICTION
National Endowment for the Arts, Fellowships/FIC-
TION
PEN American Center, Albrand Awards/NONFIC-
TION
The Mary Roberts Rinehart Fund/NONFICTION
The San Francisco Foundation/FICTION
Stanford University/FICTION
University of New Mexico/FICTION
Virginia Quarterly Review/FICTION

Children's Books

American Library Association
Association for Library Service to Children
50 East Huron Street
Chicago, IL 60611
(312) 944-6780

Program/Award: Randolph Caldecott Medal; John Newbery
Medal
Description: The Caldecott Medal is given in recognition of the
most distinguished American picture book for children. The
Newbery Medal is given in recognition of the most distin-
guished contribution to American literature for children.
Restrictions: Applicants must be U.S. citizens or residents; books
must have been published in the U.S. during the preceding
year.
Type of art: Children's Literature
$ given: Medal; no cash
Number of awards: 1 Caldecott Medal, 1 Newbery Medal
Contact: Executive Director, ALSC
Application information: Write for guidelines and list of judges.
Deadline: None; committee meets in midwinter to determine
winners.

The Boston Globe
135 Morrissey Boulevard
Boston, MA 02107
(617) 929-2649

Program/Award: The Boston Globe—Horn Book Award
Description: Annual children's book awards competition. Three cash awards are made for (1) original fiction or poetry, (2) illustration, and (3) prose nonfiction for children. The excellence of the entire book will be considered for the award. Text and illustrative material will be evaluated as they work together. Winning entries are featured at the Boston Globe Book Festival.
Restrictions: Each publisher may submit from its juvenile list no more than 10 books. The category or categories must be designated on a card for each book submitted. No textbooks. No revised editions. No manuscripts. Books must have been published in the U.S. between July 1 of the previous year and June 30 of the current award year. Judges are not restricted to books submitted by publishers.
Type of art: Children's Literature
$ given: $500 per award
Number of awards: 3 awards (1 per category) per year
Contact: Stephanie Loer, Children's Book Editor
Application information: A copy of each book entered should be mailed directly to each of the three judges, whose names and addresses are available upon request. Also, send one copy to the Boston Globe—Horn Book Award, Public Affairs Department, and one copy to Stephanie Loer, Boston Globe Children's Book Editor, 298 North Street, Medfield MA 02052.
Deadline: May 1

International Reading Association
P.O. Box 8139
800 Barksdale Road
Newark, DE 19714-8139
(302) 731-1600

Program/Award: IRA Children's Book Awards

Description: Award given in each of two categories for a first and second book, either fiction or nonfiction, by an author who shows unusual promise in the children's book field. One category is for younger readers (ages 4–10); 1 category is for older readers (ages 10–16+).

Restrictions: Books may be from any country and in any language, so long as they are copyrighted during the year of the award.

Type of art: Children's Literature

$ given: $1,000 per award

Number of awards: 2 annually

Contact: Public Information Officer

Application information: Name and address of selection committee chairman is available on request.

Deadline: December 1

Society of Children's Book Writers
P.O. Box 66296
Mar Vista Station
Los Angeles, CA 90066
(818) 347-2849

Program/Award: Golden Kite Award

Description: Three annual awards for the best children's books in the categories of fiction, nonfiction, and illustration.

Restrictions: Books must be written or illustrated by members of the Society and published in the previous calendar year.

Type of art: Children's Literature

$ given: No cash; statue and plaque

Number of awards: 3 total, 1 in each category

Contact: Sue Alexander

Application information: Write for guidelines.

Deadline: December 15

Society of Children's Book Writers
P.O. Box 66296
Mar Vista Station
Los Angeles, CA 90066
(818) 347-2849

Program/Award: Work-in-Progress Grants; Don Freeman Memorial Grant-in-Aid
Description: Work-in-Progress grants help children's book writers to complete specific projects. The Freeman Grant, given to further the recipient's understanding, training, and/or work in any aspect of the picture-book genre, funds the purchase of necessary materials, enrollment in illustrators' or writers' workshops or conferences, courses in advanced illustrating or writing techniques, and travel for research.
Restrictions: Both grants are available only to full and associate members of the Society of Children's Book Writers (SCBW).
Type of art: Children's Literature
$ given: Work-in-Progress grants are $2,000 each, with $500 for each runner-up; The Freeman grant is $1,000
Number of awards: 5 annually (2 Work-in-Progress; 2 runner-up; 1 Freeman). The Grant Committee reserves the right to withhold grants for any given year.
Contact: Grant Coordinator
Application information: Write for application forms; send SASE to appropriate grant coordinator. For Work-in-Progress grants, complete and return 3 copies of Grant Application; enclose 3 clearly reproduced copies of a synopsis of work-in-progress and a 2- to 10-page writing sample from that work. For the Freeman grant, complete and return 4 copies of Grant Application; enclose either (1) rough picture-book dummy, the picture book text in manuscript form, and 2 finished illustrations (color or black-and-white), or (2) 10 finished illustrations suitable for portfolio presentation expressly intended for picture books.
Deadline: Work-in-Progress, apply between February 1 and June 1; notification the following September. Freeman grant, apply between October 1 and November 1; notification the following March 1

Translation

The Translation Center
412 Dodge Hall
Columbia University
New York, NY 10027
(212) 854-2305

Description: Several awards for translations from all languages into English. Specific awards exist for translations from French Canadian, Dutch, Hungarian, and Italian.

Restrictions: Entries must have indication of serious intent from a publisher—may be expressed through option letter, contract, or letter from publisher stating that the work is under serious consideration. Work published up to 2 years prior to making application to Translation Center is also eligible.

Type of art: Literary Translation
$ given: $1,000 to $2,000 per award
Number of awards: 10 awards annually
Contact: Awards Secretary
Application information: All inquiries should include SASE.
Deadline: January 15, with notification by June 30

Visual Arts

General

Art Matters
P.O. Box 1428
New York, NY 10011
(212) 929-7190

Program/Award: Awards to Individuals
Description: Funds to aid individual artists in ongoing, unrestricted, project-specific visual art work and performance work with a strong visual emphasis.
Restrictions: N/A
Type of art: Visual Art, Performance Art, Multimedia Installation, Artists' Books

$ given: $1,000 to $5,000 per grant
Number of awards: Approx. 41 per year
Contact: Laura Donnelly, President; Marianne Weems, Administrator
Application information: Write to request application form.
Deadline: N/A, with notification within 2 months of application

Artpark
P.O. Box 371
Lewiston, NY 14092
(716) 745-3377

Program/Award: Visual Artists Residency
Description: Residency in upstate New York art community; residents conduct workshops.
Restrictions: N/A
Type of art: Visual Art
$ given: $325 fee and $150 living stipend per week of residency, plus round-trip travel to Lewiston
Number of awards: N/A
Contact: Joan McDonough
Application information: Submit brief proposal of work to be done, specifying visual arts category; 5–8 slides of current work; résumé; budget; and SASE.
Deadline: Usually end of October

Dallas Museum of Art
1717 North Harwood
Dallas, TX 75201
(214) 922-0220

Program/Award: Otis and Velma Davis Dozier Travel Grant
Description: Travel grant for professional visual artist.
Restrictions: Applicant must be professional artist at least 30 years old who has lived in Texas for the past three years.
Type of art: Visual Art
$ given: $6,000
Number of awards: 1
Contact: Curator of Contemporary Art

Application information: Write for guidelines.
Deadline: March 1, with notification mid-May

Fondation des Etats-Unis
15, boulevard Jourdan
75014 Paris, France
(1) 45.89.35.79

Program/Award: Harriet Hale Woolley Scholarships
Description: 9-month non-renewable scholarships for study of
   art and music in Paris at the Beaux-Arts or the Conservatoire
   National or with private instructors with approval of authori-
   ties in Paris. Recipients live at U.S. House in the Cité Interna-
   tionale and take part in its cultural activities.
Restrictions: Limited to U.S. citizens between ages 21–30, un-
   married, with college degrees or equivalents in their fields of
   study.
Type of art: Visual Art, Music
$ given: $6,000 per scholarship
Number of awards: 5 awards for the year 1989–90
Contact: Terence Murphy, Director
Application information: Make application to the address above,
   accompanied by 7 international postal coupons.
Deadline: January 31

Mid-Hudson Art Dealers Association, Inc.
25 Garden Circle
Saugerties, NY 12477
(914) 246-9100

Program/Award: Media Category Awards
Description: Purchase awards to assist visual artists.
Restrictions: Open to all artists, age 18 or older, working or
   studying in the U.S. or Canada.
Type of art: Visual Art (all media)
$ given: Up to $1,000 per award
Number of awards: 15 awards in 1984

Contact: N/A
Application information: To be placed on the information mailing list, send current address and résumé to address above.

National Academy of Design
1083 Fifth Avenue
New York, NY 10128
(212) 369-4880

Program/Award: Annual Exhibition of the National Academy of Design
Description: Exhibition of art and possible cash awards. Open juried exhibition in even-numbered years, with 250 pieces accepted; members-only exhibition in odd-numbered years, with 200 pieces accepted.
Restrictions: Original works in oil, watercolor, tempera, casein, and pastels, as well as sculpture, drawing, and prints in any medium are eligible. Works previously exhibited in the National Academy Galleries are not eligible.
Type of art: Visual Art
$ given: $200 to $3,000 per award
Number of awards: 50 awards for 1990
Contact: Barbara S. Krulik, Assistant Director
Application information: Prospectus and entry cards (usually available from mid-October) may be obtained by writing to Annual Exhibition, National Academy of Design. Juries of Selection and Award Judge the actual artwork; slides are not acceptable.
Deadline: Receiving Day is usually in early January, with notification the end of January

National Endowment for the Arts
1100 Pennsylvania Avenue, NW
Washington, DC 20506
(202) 682-5444

Program/Award: Inter-Arts Program
Description: Several categories of funding, mostly for organiza-

tions, artist communities, and service organizations, but also for individual artists' projects that result in the creation of original work that challenges the traditional arts disciplines.
Restrictions: The program is open to artists' projects involving innovative work and to the collaboration of artists of different disciplines or new technologies.
Type of art: Multidisciplinary
$ given: Usually ranging from $5,000 to $15,000 per grant, with a few grants exceeding $35,000. Matching funds requirement, 1 to 1.
Number of awards: Varies; 240 awards (in all categories) in fiscal year 1988
Contact: Joel Snyder, Acting Director, Inter-Arts Program
Application information: Write for application guidelines and deadlines.

National Endowment for the Arts
Visual Arts Program
Room 729
1100 Pennsylvania Avenue, NW
Washington, DC 20506
(202) 682-5448

Program/Award: Visual Arts Program
Description: Assistance through fellowships to individual artists; also a few matching grants to organizations. Categories: (1) Visual Artists Fellowships; (2) Visual Artists Organizations; (3) Art in Public Places (support for commissions); (4) Visual Artists Forums (support for discourses); (5) Special Projects (for innovative, model projects).
Restrictions: Limited to practicing professional artists of exceptional talent and demonstrated ability in chosen media. Individuals may apply only once, and in one fellowship area, during any 2-year fellowship cycle. Applicants must be U.S. citizens or permanent residents.
Type of art: Painting, Sculpture, Photography, Crafts, Printmaking, Drawing, Artists' Books, Video, Conceptual Art, Performance Art, and new genres
$ given: Visual Artists Fellowships, $5,000 to $20,000 each, based

on specific review criteria; Art in Public Places, $5,000 to $50,000 each

Number of awards: 390 awards (in all categories) in fiscal year 1990

Contact: N/A

Application information: Call for guidelines and application forms.

Deadline: Varies according to category

National Foundation for Advancement in the Arts
3915 Biscayne Boulevard
Miami, FL 33137
(305) 573-0490

Program/Award: Career Advancement of Visual Artists (CAVA)

Description: Three 4-month residencies for professional visual artists.

Restrictions: Open to visual artists in all media, ages 18–40, who have worked at least one year as professionals.

Type of art: Visual Art (all media)

$ given: $5,000 stipend for personal expenses and art supplies, plus studio and living accommodations

Number of awards: 3 per year

Contact: William Banchs, Director of Program Development

Application information: Application form available from NFAA after May 1. NFAA resident fellows are chosen by a jury of nationally recognized professionals. CAVA is renewable annually for a total of 3 years.

Deadline: October 1

Southeastern Center for Contemporary Art
750 Marguerite Drive
Winston-Salem, NC 27106
(919) 725-1904

Program/Award: Awards in the Visual Arts (AVA)

Description: National fellowships; works of the recipients are coordinated into a museum exhibition that tours 3 cities. Fellowship lasts 3–4 months.

Restrictions: Limited to U.S. citizens. No restrictions on media.
Type of art: Visual Art (all media)
$ given: $15,000 fellowship to each artist; $5,000 grant to each museum exhibiting the AVA show
Number of awards: 10 awards to artists annually; 1 in each of 10 designated areas of the country
Contact: Virginia S. Rutter, Special Assistant
Application information: By nomination only. Not open to application. A network of 100 AVA nominators is established nationwide. Once nominated, the artist must submit 10 slides and pertinent material about his work. If a video artist, he must submit one 3/4-inch cassette with a 10-minute segment.
Deadline: July 31, with notification in November

Also see: American Academy and Institute, A-I Awards/FICTION

Painting

American Academy and Institute of Arts and Letters
633 West 155th Street
New York, NY 10032
(212) 368-5900

Program/Award: Louise Nevelson Award in Art
Description: Annual award given in rotation to a sculptor, a painter, or a printmaker.
Restrictions: N/A
Type of art: Painting, Sculpture, Printmaking
$ given: $5,000 per award
Number of awards: 1 annually
Contact: Lydia Kaim, Assistant to Executive Director
Application information: No applications may be submitted. By nomination from the membership only.

American Academy and Institute of Arts and Letters
633 West 155th Street
New York, NY 10032
(212) 368-5900

Program/Award: Richard and Hinda Rosenthal Foundation Awards
Description: Annual award for American work of fiction published during preceding 12 months. A second annual award to a younger American painter of distinction who has not yet been accorded due recognition.
Restrictions: N/A
Type of art: Fiction, Painting
$ given: $5,000 per award
Number of awards: 1 annually in each category
Contact: Lydia Kaim, Assistant to Executive Director
Application information: No applications may be submitted. Nomination by the membership only.

American Watercolor Society
47 Fifth Avenue
New York, NY 10003
(212) 206-8986

Description: Awards for watercolors accepted in the Society's annual exhibition. Also, scholarships for the study of watercolor painting. Traveling exhibitions.
Restrictions: Paintings must be submitted for the exhibition; paintings must be aquamedia on paper, unvarnished. One submission per artist only.
Type of art: Painting
$ given: Exhibition awards total approx. $20,000 annually with 9 medals. $1,600 Gold Medal; $1,500 Silver Medal; $1,200 Bronze Medal
Number of awards: 30 exhibition awards annually
Contact: Exhibition Secretary
Application information: Detailed instructions for submitting works to the exhibition are available on request. Submissions juried.

The Foothills Art Center, Inc.
809 15th Street
Golden, CO 80401
(303) 279-3922

Program/Award: Rocky Mountain National Watermedia Exhibition
Description: Cash awards for watermedia paintings.
Restrictions: Open to all artists living in the U.S.
Type of art: Painting
$ given: $9,000 in total support
Number of awards: 20 per exhibition
Contact: Marian Metsopoulos, Executive Director
Application information: Send SASE for entry form and deadline information.

Francis J. Greenburger Foundation
55 Fifth Avenue
New York, NY 10003
(212) 206-6092

Program/Award: Francis J. Greenburger Award
Description: Award given to artists of extraordinary merit who are not well known to the public.
Restrictions: N/A
Type of art: Sculpture, Painting
$ given: $6,000 per award
Number of awards: 5 per year
Contact: George W. Hofmann, Executive Director; Carol Frederick, Assistant Director
Application information: Applications are not accepted; by nomination only.

Also see: American Academy in Rome/ARCHITECTURE
Education Studio Museum in Harlem/PRINTMAKING
Fine Arts Work Center in Provincetown/SCULPTURE
The Gottlieb Foundation, Emergency Assistance/SCULPTURE

The Gottlieb Foundation, General Support/SCULP-
TURE
The Elizabeth Greenshields Foundation/PRINTMAK-
ING
Institute of International Education, Cintas/PRINT-
MAKING
Pollock-Krasner Foundation/PRINTMAKING

Sculpture

Creative Glass Center of America
Wheaton Village
Glasstown Road
Millville, NJ 08332
(609) 825-6800

Program/Award: Creative Glass Center of America Fellowship
Program
Description: Funding, housing, and use of CGCA glassblowing
facility.
Restrictions: Limited to U.S. citizens. Applicants must have prior
experience in glasswork and must reside at or near site during
fellowship period.
Type of art: Sculpture, Visual Art
$ given: $750 per fellowship plus housing and use of CGCA
glassblowing facility
Number of awards: 8 annually; 4 for February through June, 4
for July through November
Contact: Karl C. Hensel, Managing Director
Application information: Write for guidelines and forms. Submit completed application form with 10 slides of work, statement of intent, and 2 letters of recommendation.

Fine Arts Work Center in Provincetown, Inc.
24 Pearl Street
P.O. Box 565
Provincetown, MA 02657
(508) 487-9960

Description: Fellowships, lodging, and studio space, and a community situation in which to develop art. Resident staff available to fellows, as well as a program of visiting artists. Residency runs for 7 months, October through April.

Restrictions: Limited to painters, sculptors, and creative writers who have spent time working on their own and have created a considerable body of work which can be presented in the form of slides or manuscripts.

Type of art: Painting, Sculpture, Creative Writing

$ given: $3,500 stipend per residency plus private living space and working studio in Provincetown, Massachusetts

Number of awards: 20 annually

Contact: Director

Application information: Forms and application information may be requested from the above address. Application fee of $20.

Deadline: February 1, with notification May 1

The Foothills Art Center, Inc.
809 15th Street
Golden, CO 80401
(303) 279-3922

Program/Award: North American Sculpture Exhibition
Description: Cash awards for sculpture.
Restrictions: Limited to residents of U.S., Canada, and Mexico.
Type of art: Sculpture
$ given: $6,000 in total support
Number of awards: 8 per exhibition
Contact: Marian Metsopoulos, Executive Director
Application information: Send SASE to address above for entry form and deadline information.

Adolph and Esther Gottlieb Foundation, Inc.
380 West Broadway
New York, NY 10012
(212) 226-0581

Program/Award: Emergency Assistance Program
Description: Cash awards to mature creative painters and sculp-

tors who are experiencing financial hardship resulting from a current or recent emergency.

Restrictions: Applicant must be able to demonstrate a minimum involvement of 10 years in a mature phase of his or her work; need must result from current or recent emergency beyond the artist's usual circumstances.

Type of art: Painting, Sculpture

$ given: Varies; maximum of $5,000 per award

Number of awards: Varies

Contact: Sanford Hirsch, Administrator

Application information: One-time support. Obtain further information from address above.

Adolph and Esther Gottlieb Foundation, Inc.
380 West Broadway
New York, NY 10012
(212) 226-0581

Program/Award: General Support Program

Description: Cash awards to mature creative painters and sculptors who have been involved with a mature phase of their art for at least 20 years, and are in current financial need.

Restrictions: No support for projects, groups, or organizations. See Description for restrictions on individual applicants.

Type of art: Painting, Sculpture

$ given: $12,500 average per award

Number of awards: Varies; 10 for the year 1989

Contact: Sanford Hirsch, Administrator

Application information: Written requests for applications must be from prospective applicants only. New application necessary each year—no automatic renewal of funding. Visual materials must be submitted in addition to completed application form.

Deadline: December 15, with notification in early March

Also see: American Academy and Institute, Nevelson Award/
      PAINTING
      American Academy in Rome/ARCHITECTURE
      Ball State University Art Gallery/DRAWING

Education Studio Museum in Harlem/PRINTMAK-
ING
Francis J. Greenburger Foundation/PAINTING
The Elizabeth Greenshields Foundation/PRINTMAK-
ING
Institute of International Education, Cintas/PRINT-
MAKING
John Michael Kohler Arts Center/CRAFTS/FOLK
ART
Pollock-Krasner Foundation/PRINTMAKING

Drawing

Ball State University Art Gallery
College of Fine Arts
Ball State University
Muncie, IN 47306
(317) 285-5242

Program/Award: Annual Drawing and Small Sculpture Show
Description: Financial support to emerging artists provided
   through prize monies awarded in conjunction with annual
   competitive exhibition.
Restrictions: Limited to U.S. residents.
Type of art: Drawing, Sculpture
$ given: $500 per award
Number of awards: 4 annually
Contact: Alain Joyaux, Director
Application information: Prospectus available in spring of each
   year. Exhibition is juried; awards are made by the juror each
   year.
Deadline: Approx. May 15, with notification by end of summer

Also see: The Elizabeth Greenshields Foundation/PRINTMAK-
   ING

Printmaking

Education Studio Museum in Harlem
144 West 125th Street
New York, NY 10027
(212) 864-4500

Program/Award: Artists-in-Residence Program
Description: Funding and studio space for visual artists.
Restrictions: Applicants must be minority artists (Black, Hispanic, Asian, Native American, etc.).
Type of art: Painting, Printmaking, Sculpture, Visual Art (General)
$ given: $10,000 stipend and $200 for art supplies per artist, plus studio space at the Museum
Number of awards: 3 per year
Contact: Stanley Tarver, Director of Education
Application information: Write or call for application form. Submit completed form with résumé and 10–12 slides of work.
Deadline: Early May for October–September program period

The Elizabeth Greenshields Foundation
1814 Sherbrooke Street West
Montreal, PQ H3H 1E4, Canada
(514) 937-9225

Program/Award: The Elizabeth Greenshields Foundation Grants
Description: Financial aid for talented young artists in early stages of their careers.
Restrictions: Applicants must be under 31 years old and have already started or completed training in an established school of art; work must be representational or figurative (abstract art is precluded by the Foundation's charter).
Type of art: Painting, Sculpture, Printmaking, Drawing
$ given: $8,000 (Canadian) per award
Number of awards: 45 awards in 1990
Contact: Patricia Graham, Treasurer
Application information: Write directly to the Foundation for an

application form. Grants are made directly to the beneficiaries, not through other organizations.
Deadline: None

Institute of International Education
Arts International Program
809 United Nations Plaza
New York, NY 10017–3580
(212) 984-5564

Program/Award: Cintas Fellowships in the Arts
Description: Fellowships awarded to persons of Cuban citizenship or lineage for achievement of a creative nature. The fellowship runs for 12 months, September 1 through August 31.
Restrictions: Limited to young professionals in the creative arts, of Cuban citizenship or lineage, who can give evidence of their creative production by records of exhibitions, performances, or published books or scores. Students not eligible, nor are performing artists. No fixed age limit, but preference for young artists who have completed academic and technical training.
Type of art: Architecture, Painting, Sculpture, Printmaking, Music Composition, Creative Writing
$ given: $10,000 per fellowship, paid in 4 quarterly stipends
Number of awards: 6 or more fellowships annually
Contact: Rebecca A. Abrams, Associate Programs Officer
Application information: Eligible candidates may request application and letter of reference forms. Applications should be in English and should be accompanied by supporting documentation of appropriate nature, such as published books or scores, photos or color slides of paintings or sculpture.
Deadline: Applications accepted between January 1 and March 1, with notification in June

Pollock-Krasner Foundation, Inc.
P.O. Box 4957
New York, NY 10185
(212) 517-5400

Program/Award: Pollock-Krasner Foundation Grant

Description: Grant for individuals of high artistic merit and financial need.
Restrictions: N/A
Type of art: Painting, Printmaking, Sculpture, Visual Art (General)
$ given: Depends upon financial needs of the artist
Number of awards: N/A
Contact: Charles C. Bergman, Executive Vice President
Application information: Write for guidelines and forms.
Deadline: None; ongoing funding

Also see: American Academy and Institute, Nevelson Award/
PAINTING
The Print Club/PHOTOGRAPHY
The San Francisco Foundation/PHOTOGRAPHY

Photography

The Center for Photography at Woodstock
59 Tinker Street
Woodstock, NY 12498
(914) 679-9957

Program/Award: The Photographers' Fund
Description: The Fund makes annual awards to regional photographers of vision and talent, selected by portfolio review by a panel of 3 noted national artists.
Restrictions: Limited to residents of 18 upstate New York counties (Albany, Columbia, Delaware, Dutchess, Fulton, Greene, Hamilton, Montgomery, Orange, Otsego, Rensselaer, Saratoga, Schenectady, Schoharie, Sullivan, Ulster, Warren, and Washington).
Type of art: Photography
$ given: $1,000 per award
Number of awards: 3 annually
Contact: Director
Application information: Call Center for application procedure.

The Friends of Photography
250 Fourth Street
San Francisco, CA 94103
(415) 391-7500

Program/Award: Ferguson Award
Description: Cash award presented to photographer who has demonstrated evidence of notable achievement and continuing serious commitment to the medium.
Restrictions: Photographers of any age, race, nationality, or aesthetic persuasion are eligible.
Type of art: Photography
$ given: $2,000 per award
Number of awards: 1 annually
Contact: David Featherstone, Director of Publications
Application information: Grant guidelines and instructions are available in February of each year. Applications are accepted during a 2-week period each spring. Specific dates vary year to year. Send SASE for details.

The Friends of Photography
250 Fourth Street
San Francisco, CA 94103
(415) 391-7500

Program/Award: Ruttenberg Foundation Award
Description: Cash award to emerging artist who concentrates on portraiture in the context of fine art photography.
Restrictions: N/A
Type of art: Photography
$ given: $2,000 per award
Number of awards: 1 annually
Contact: David Featherstone, Director of Publications
Application information: Guidelines available in January. Send SASE for grant guidelines and application form.

Light Work
316 Waverly Avenue
Syracuse, NY 13244
(315) 443-2450 or 443-1300

Program/Award: Light Work Artist-in-Residency Program
Description: Artists-in-residence program and funding for exhibitions.
Restrictions: Applicants must be working photographic artists with 10 or more years of experience.
Type of art: Photography
$ given: Artists-in-residence receive $1,200 plus use of private darkroom and apartment in Syracuse for one month. Funding for exhibitions averages $300 per exhibition.
Number of awards: 12–15 artists in residency per year; 9 artists receive funding for exhibits
Contact: Jeffrey Hoone, Director
Application information: Write for details.
Deadline: None; ongoing funding

Photographic Resource Center
602 Commonwealth Avenue
Boston, MA 02215
(617) 353-0700

Program/Award: The Leopold Godowsky, Jr., Color Photography Award
Description: Award given every 18 months to outstanding color photographers worldwide.
Restrictions: N/A
Type of art: Photography
$ given: $5,000 per award
Number of awards: N/A
Contact: Stan Trecker, Executive Director
Application information: Applications are not accepted; nomination is by jury of members.

The Print Club
1614 Latimer Street
Philadelphia, PA 19103–6398
(215) 735-6090

Program/Award: The Print Club's Annual International Competition

Description: Prizes through international competition; cash or purchase prizes for prints or photographs submitted to a jury. Works become part of the permanent collection at the Philadelphia Museum of Art.

Restrictions: Limited to original work done within the last 2 years. Artist pays $25 membership fee, entitling member to services of the Print Club, such as referrals.

Type of art: Photography, Printmaking
$ given: $250 to $1,000 per prize
Number of awards: 18 prizes in 1990
Contact: Anne Schuster, Director
Application information: Specific information available each year in August. Competition is held in September/October. Exhibitions held in November (prints) and January (photos). Prizes are awarded during September/October.
Deadline: Early fall

The San Francisco Foundation
685 Market Street
Suite 910
San Francisco, CA 94105
(415) 543-0223

Program/Award: James D. Phelan Awards in Art

Description: Awards to young California artists in various fields of art; 3 awards each offered in printmaking and photography one year, in film and video the next.

Restrictions: Limited to native-born Californians.
Type of art: Printmaking, Photography, Film, Video
$ given: $2,500 per award
Number of awards: 6 per year

Contact: N/A
Application information: Write to request details.

Crafts/Folk Art

Craft Emergency Relief Fund
1000 Connecticut Avenue, Suite 9
Washington, DC 20036
(413) 625-9672

Program/Award: Emergency Loan
Description: Last-resort loans for craftspersons needing emergency funding.
Restrictions: Applicants must be craftspersons working fulltime, who have experienced an emergency situation that interrupts their work. Reapplication allowed.
Type of art: Crafts
$ given: $200 to $450 per interest-free loan; no specified repayment schedule
Number of awards: N/A
Contact: Lois Ahrens, Director
Application information: Write for application form and guidelines.
Deadline: None; ongoing funding, with notification within one week after application

John Michael Kohler Arts Center
608 New York Avenue
P.O. Box 489
Sheboygan, WI 53082–0489
(414) 458-6144

Program/Award: Arts/Industry Residency
Description: 2- to 6-month residency with honorarium, housing, and paid round-trip air fare for sculptors and craftspersons, as well as artists interested in working in another medium.
Restrictions: Open to artists age 18 and older.
Type of art: Sculpture, Ceramic Art, Crafts

$ given: $100/week honorarium plus housing for period of residency and paid round-trip air fare

Number of awards: 6 artists receive residencies of 2–6 months each

Contact: N/A

Application information: Send résumé, 20 slides, statement about work, 1-page proposal for residency, simple drawings of proposed project, and time required for residency.

Deadline: Rotating review of applications

All Arts Disciplines

American Academy and Institute of Arts and Letters
633 West 155th Street
New York, NY 10032
(212) 368-5900

Program/Award: The Award for Distinguished Service to the Arts

Description: Award granted periodically to acknowledge individuals who have, by their artistic production in any genre, exerted an important influence.

Restrictions: Limited to U.S. citizens who are not members of the Academy and Institute.

Type of art: All Disciplines

$ given: Citation plus $1,000 or more, at the discretion of the Board

Number of awards: N/A

Contact: Lydia Kaim, Assistant to Executive Director

Application information: No applications may be submitted. By nomination from the membership only.

Change Inc.
P.O. Box 705
Cooper Station
New York, NY 10276
(212) 473-3742

Description: Emergency grants to professional artists in all fields. Eviction, utility turn-off, medical expenses, fire and theft losses constitute emergencies.
Restrictions: Applicants must be professional artists, individually destitute; must explain why no other funds are available.
Type of art: All Disciplines
$ given: $100 to $500 per grant
Number of awards: N/A
Contact: N/A
Application information: Applicants must submit detailed letters, proof of being artists (slides, résumé, exhibition announcements, reviews of work), at least 2 letters of reference, copies of bills, and specific amount needed. One-time grant.
Deadline: None, with notification within 2 weeks of receipt of application

John Simon Guggenheim Memorial Foundation
90 Park Avenue
New York, NY 10016
(212) 687-4470

Program/Award: Fellowships to Assist Research and Artistic Creation
Description: Fellowships for scholars and artists in any field of knowledge and creation in any of the arts, to engage in research or artistic creation under the freest possible conditions.
Restrictions: Awarded to men and women of high intellectual and personal qualifications who have already demonstrated unusual capacity for productive scholarship or unusual creative ability in the arts. Fellows are usually 30–45 years of age, but there are no age restrictions. Fellowships are awarded through 2 annual competitions: one open to citizens and permanent residents of the U.S. and Canada; the other open to

citizens and permanent residents of Latin America and the Caribbean. Awarded by the Trustees upon nominations made by a Committee of Selection. Guggenheim Fellowships may not be held concurrently with other fellowships.

Type of art: All Disciplines

$ given: $24,000 average award; amount adjusted to needs and resources of individual Fellows, and the scope of their plans

Number of awards: 143 for the year 1990

Contact: Fellowship Program

Application information: Write for official application materials.

Deadline: October 1 for U.S./Canada; December 1 for Latin America/Caribbean. Notification: March for U.S./Canada; June for Latin America/Caribbean.

Lyndhurst Foundation
Suite 701, Tallan Building
100 West M. L. King Boulevard
Chattanooga, TN 37402–2561
(615) 756-0767

Description: Funding for the arts; limited to some regional, but primarily local, organizations. Awards to individuals are made only at the initiative of the Foundation, never in response to applications.

Restrictions: N/A

Type of art: All Disciplines

$ given: $20,000 to $30,000 per year

Number of awards: 60 awards, plus 24 Lyndhurst Prizes

Contact: Jack E. Murrah, Executive Director

Application information: Individuals may not apply. The Foundation's board of directors selects award recipients.

John D. and Catherine T. MacArthur Foundation
140 South Dearborn Street
Suite 700
Chicago, IL 60603
(312) 726-8000

Program/Award: The MacArthur Fellows Program

Description: Unrestricted fellowships to exceptionally talented and promising young artists who show originality, dedication to creative pursuit, and capacity for self-direction.

Restrictions: Limited to U.S. citizens.

Type of art: All Disciplines

$ given: $150,000 to $375,000 per 5-year fellowship period; exact amount based on candidate's age

Number of awards: 25 concurrently

Contact: James M. Furman, Executive Vice President

Application information: Guidelines, annual reports, and publications available upon request. No direct applications are accepted for the Fellows Program.

National Endowment for the Arts
1100 Pennsylvania Avenue, NW
Washington, DC 20506
(202) 682-5562

Program/Award: United States–Japan Artist Exchange Fellowship Program

Description: Under an exchange agreement between governments, 5 fellowships are awarded annually to Americans in the creative and performing arts. (Likewise, 5 fellowships are awarded to Japanese artists.) American Fellows spend 6 months in Japan and receive cash award and round-trip transportation.

Restrictions: Limited to U.S. citizens or permanent residents who have not been residents of Japan for more than 2 months and who have not received other grants of a similar nature. Students, scholars, and art critics are not eligible. Recipient must be able to spend 6 consecutive months in Japan.

Type of art: All Disciplines

$ given: 600,000 yen per month (for 6 months) plus round-trip transportation to Japan

Number of awards: 5 fellowships per year

Contact: Beverly Kratochvil, Program Officer, International Activities

Application information: Guidelines and application forms may be obtained by writing.

Deadline: Varies according to specific arts discipline

Northwood Institute
Alden B. Dow Creativity Center
Midland, MI 48640-2398
(517) 832-4478

Program/Award: Creativity Fellowships
Description: 10-week summer residencies to allow individuals the opportunity to pursue project ideas. Transportation to Northwood Institute, housing, food, small weekly stipend, and modest project costs included in award.
Restrictions: Applicant must be qualified in field of pursuit and have maturity to work independently and live cooperatively.
Type of art: All Fields and Professions
$ given: Residencies valued at approx. $4,000 each
Number of awards: Average of 4 residencies annually
Contact: Carol B. Coppage, Executive Director
Application information: Write or phone for application form. Include recent résumé with completed application.
Deadline: December 31, with notification April 1

Ludwig Vogelstein Foundation, Inc.
P.O. Box 4924
Brooklyn, NY 11240-4924

Description: Funding for original projects in the arts and humanities by individuals who do not have access to other sources of support.
Restrictions: Eligibility determined by need and merit. Grants given only to projects with budgets under $5,000.
Type of art: All Disciplines
$ given: Average award, $2,200
Number of awards: 26 grants in 1988
Contact: Frances Pishny, Executive Director
Application information: Write for full application procedures after January 1.
Deadline: Varies each year

II

Geographically Restricted Funding to Individuals, by State

Alabama

Alabama State Council on the Arts
One Dexter Avenue
Montgomery, AL 36130
(205) 261-4076

Description: Fellowships and technical assistance grants for Alabama artists.
Restrictions: Limited to U.S. citizens who are residents of Alabama.
Type of art: All Disciplines
$ given: $2,500 to $5,000 per fellowship; technical assistance to a maximum of $1,000 per grant
Number of awards: 12 fellowships per year; no specific limit on number of technical assistance grants
Contact: Randy Shoults, Visual Arts Coordinator
Application information: Write for application materials.
Deadline: May 1 for fellowships; technical assistance consideration ongoing

Appalshop
P.O. Box 743
Whitesburg, KY 41858
(606) 633-0108

Program/Award: Southeast Media Fellowships

Description: National Endowment for the Arts funding for regional media artists.

Restrictions: Limited to residents of Alabama, Florida, Georgia, Kentucky, Louisiana, Mississippi, North Carolina, South Carolina, Tennessee, and Virginia.

Type of art: Film, Video, Media Art

$ given: $5,000 per fellowship

Number of awards: Maximum of 15 per year

Contact: N/A

Application information: Write for guidelines and forms.

Alaska

Alaska State Council on the Arts
619 Warehouse Avenue, Suite 220
Anchorage, AK 99501
(907) 279-1558

Program/Award: Individual Artist Fellowship Program

Description: State funding for individual artists.

Restrictions: Limited to Alaska residents.

Type of art: Music Composition, Dance, Film, Painting, Photography, Printmaking, Sculpture, Creative Writing, Video Art

$ given: $5,000 per fellowship

Number of awards: N/A

Contact: Christine D'Arcy, Director, Eligibility

Application information: Write for application form.

Arizona

Arizona Commission on the Arts
417 West Roosevelt Street
Phoenix, AZ 85003
(602) 255-5882

Description: Fellowships and grants in the visual arts, performing arts, and creative writing.

Restrictions: Limited to Arizona residents age 18 and over. No students.

Type of art: Film, Photography, Playwriting, Poetry, Video Art

$ given: $400 per fellowship

Number of awards: 6 annually; 2 in film/video/photography, 2 in poetry, 2 in playwriting

Contact: Tonda Gorton, Public Information Officer

Application information: Write for Artist's Guide.

Deadline: Fall; write for specific date

Rocky Mountain Film Center
Hunter 102, P.O. Box 316
University of Colorado
Boulder, CO 80309–0316
(303) 492-1531

Program/Award: Western States Media Fellowship Program

Description: Funding to individual regional media artists. 1 year fellowship period.

Restrictions: Limited to residents of Arizona, Alaska, California, Colorado, Hawaii, Idaho, Montana, Nevada, New Mexico, Oregon, Utah, Washington, Wyoming, and the Pacific Territories. Organizations and full-time students not eligible. Funds not for script development.

Type of art: Film, Video, Media Art

$ given: $1,000 to $5,000 per fellowship; Washington State Arts Commission also awards $5,000 to the highest ranked recipient from Washington

Number of awards: N/A

Contact: Patti Bruck, Program Coordinator

Application information: Write or call for guidelines and application form.

Also see: Dallas Museum of Art, Degolyer Fund/TEXAS

Arkansas

Arkansas Arts Council
Suite 200, The Heritage Center East
225 East Markham
Little Rock, AR 72201
(501) 371-2539

Description: Fellowship grants to individuals, and funding to nonprofit organizations within the state.
Restrictions: Limited to Arkansas residents.
Type of art: Architecture, Visual Art, Theater, Creative Writing, Dance, Music, Media Art
$ given: $2,500 to $5,000 per fellowship in various disciplines, rotating annually
Number of awards: 5–10 fellowships per year
Contact: Becky Hamilton, Assistant Director of Programs
Application information: Write for Guide to Grants.
Deadline: January 15. Notification: Applications reviewed by Council in late March/early April

Friends of American Writers
506 Rose Street
Des Plaines, IL 60016
(708) 827-8339

Program/Award: Annual Book Awards
Description: 4 awards yearly for published books by a Midwestern author or with a Midwestern locale: two cash awards for adult books; two cash awards for juvenile books.
Restrictions: Author must be a current resident of one of 16 midwestern states, or have lived there for at least 5 years, or have set the book in the region. States include Arkansas, Illinois, Indiana, Iowa, Kansas, Kentucky, Michigan, Minnesota, Missouri, Nebraska, North Dakota, Ohio, Oklahoma, South Dakota, Tennessee, and Wisconsin. Eligible authors shall not have published more than 3 books in the field and shall not have received a previous monetary award of $1,000 or more. Books must have been published within the calendar year of the award.

Type of art: Fiction, Nonfiction
$ given: Adult books, $1,200 First Prize, $750 Second Prize. Juvenile books, $700 First Prize, $400 Second Prize
Number of awards: 4 annually
Contact: Vivian Mortensen, Awards Chairman
Application information: No application necessary. Send 2 copies of the book to the Awards Chairman.
Deadline: December 1, with notification in April

Mid-America Arts Alliance
912 Baltimore Avenue, Suite 700
Kansas City, MO 64105
(816) 421-1388

Program/Award: Regional Fellowships for Visual Artists
Description: Fellowships to individual regional visual artists.
Restrictions: Limited to U.S. citizens who are residents of Arkansas, Kansas, Missouri, Nebraska, Oklahoma, or Texas. Applicants must be professional artists.
Type of art: Visual Art
$ given: $5,000 per fellowship
Number of awards: 15–20 per year
Contact: Edeen Martin, Director of Visual Arts
Application information: Write for application materials.

California

California Arts Council
601 North 7th Street
Suite 100
Sacramento, CA 95814
(916) 445-1530

Program/Award: Artists in Residence; Individual Artists Fellowships; Art in Public Buildings
Description: The CAC has a total of 7 funding program categories, of which 3 are for individuals and provide residencies, fellowships, and exhibitions.
Restrictions: Limited to California residents.

Type of art: All Disciplines
$ given: $10 million annual budget for all 7 categories of funding
Number of awards: 1,200 awards in all categories
Contact: JoAnn M. Anglin, Public Information Officer
Application information: Write for application guidelines and
   deadlines.

Dewar's Young Artists Recognition Awards
10250 Santa Monica Boulevard, Suite 194
Los Angeles, CA 90067

Program/Award: Dewar's Young Artists Awards
Description: Grants to individual poets.
Restrictions: Limited to California residents.
Type of art: Poetry
$ given: $2,000 per grant
Number of awards: Total of 10 per year in 5 categories
Contact: N/A
Application information: Write for guidelines.

Film Arts Foundation
346 Ninth Street, 2nd Floor
San Francisco, CA 94013
(415) 552-8760

Program/Award: Film Arts Foundation Grants Program
Description: Grants to film and video artists.
Restrictions: Limited to U.S. citizens who are residents of the San
   Francisco Bay Area (Alameda, Contra Costa, Marin, Napa,
   Santa Clara, Santa Cruz, San Mateo, Solano, and Sonoma
   counties).
Type of art: Film, Video
$ given: $1,000 to $5,000 per grant
Number of awards: N/A
Contact: Gail Silva, Director
Application information: Write for guidelines and application
   materials.

Fleishhacker Foundation
One Maritime Plaza, Suite 830
San Francisco, CA 94111
(415) 788-2909

Program/Award: The Eureka Fellowship Program
Description: Fellowships for individual artists in the Bay Area to allow them to spend uninterrupted time pursuing creative work. The time may be used to begin or complete a specific project, to explore new directions or techniques, or to continue to develop work already in progress.
Restrictions: Limited to residents of Alameda, Contra Costa, Marin, San Mateo, Santa Clara, and San Francisco counties of California. Applicants must be at least 25 years of age. Full-time and part-time students are not eligible.
Type of art: Visual Art (specific disciplines rotate annually)
$ given: $15,000 per fellowship, paid in equal monthly installments; intended to cover basic living expenses for a 1-year period
Number of awards: N/A
Contact: Sarah S. Lutman, Executive Director
Application information: Write for guidelines and application materials.
Deadline: September 15

The San Francisco Foundation
685 Market Street
Suite 910
San Francisco, CA 94105
(415) 543-0223

Program/Award: Joseph Henry Jackson Award in Literature; James D. Phelan Award in Literature
Description: Awards to the authors of unpublished, partly completed, book-length works of fiction, nonfiction, short stories, or poetry (Phelan Award includes drama as well). Additionally, a special fund has been donated by Mary Tanenbaum in memory of J. H. Jackson to encourage the writing of nonfiction. From this fund, an award may be made for a manuscript

of nonfiction submitted in either the Jackson or Phelan competitions, but not selected to receive either of these awards.
Restrictions: Applicants for the Jackson Award must have been residents of northern California or Nevada for the 3 consecutive years prior to January 15 of the award year. Applicants for the Phelan Award must be native-born Californians. For all awards, applicants must be between ages 20–35 on January 15 of the award year. Their writings need not concern California. Applicants may compete for both awards and in more than one type of literature, but may win only one award. A single manuscript and application will serve for both awards (if the applicant is eligible for both competitions).
Type of art: Fiction, Nonfiction, Short Story, Poetry, Drama
$ given: $2,000 per Jackson or Phelan award; $1,000 per special fund award
Number of awards: 1 of each annually
Contact: Awards Office
Application information: Write for official application forms after November 1.
Deadline: January 15, with notification by June 15

The San Francisco Foundation
685 Market Street
Suite 910
San Francisco, CA 94105
(415) 543-0223

Program/Award: James D. Phelan Awards in Art
Description: Awards to young California artists in various fields of art. Three awards each offered in printmaking and photography one year; in film and video the next year.
Restrictions: Limited to native-born Californians.
Type of art: Printmaking, Photography, Film, Video
$ given: $2,500 per award
Number of awards: 6 per year
Contact: N/A
Application information: Write to request guidelines.

Also see: Rocky Mountain Film Center/ARIZONA

Colorado

Colorado Council on the Arts and Humanities
770 Pennsylvania Street
Denver, CO 80203
(303) 866-5428

Program/Award: Creative Fellowships
Description: Fellowships for individual Colorado artists.
Restrictions: Limited to U.S. citizens who are residents of Colorado.
Type of art: All Disciplines
$ given: $4,000 per fellowship
Number of awards: 8 annually
Contact: Gail M. Goldman, Director, Individual Artist Programs
Application information: Write for guidelines.
Deadline: November 15

Also see: Dallas Museum of Art, Degolyer Fund/TEXAS
Rocky Mountain Film Center/ARIZONA

Connecticut

Arts Extension Service, Division of Continuing Education
Goodell Building
University of Massachusetts
Amherst, MA 01003
(413) 545-2360

Program/Award: New England Film Festival
Description: Annual film festival.
Restrictions: Limited to residents of Connecticut, Massachusetts, Maine, New Hampshire, Rhode Island, and Vermont—or students who completed their films while at colleges in those 6 states.
Type of art: Film
$ given: $1,000 for Boston Globe Best of Festival award; 4 awards totaling $2,000 to students and independent filmmakers; plus honorable mentions
Number of awards: Minimum of 5 annually

Contact: N/A
Application information: Write for guidelines and application materials.

Boston Film and Video Foundation
1126 Boylston
Boston, MA 02215
(617) 536-1540

Program/Award: New England Film/Video Fellowship Program
Description: Fellowships for individual filmmakers and video artists.
Restrictions: Limited to U.S. citizens who are residents of Connecticut, Massachusetts, Maine, New Hampshire, Rhode Island, and Vermont. Must be over age 18 and must remain in the New England region during the fellowship period. No organizations or collaborative groups; noncommercial projects only. No full-time students or projects associated with a degree program.
Type of art: Film, Video
$ given: $5,000 per fellowship to complete work-in-progress or new work; plus facility and equipment usage worth up to $5,000
Number of awards: N/A
Contact: N/A
Application information: Write for guidelines and application materials.

Connecticut Commission on the Arts
227 Lawrence Street
Hartford, CT 06106
(203) 566-4770

Program/Award: Individual Artists Project Grants
Description: Project grants for new works by individual Connecticut artists.
Restrictions: Limited to Connecticut residents.
Type of art: Dance, Creative Writing, Visual Art
$ given: Up to $5,000 per grant

Number of awards: N/A
Contact: Tony Norris, Public Information Officer
Application information: Call for information.

Delaware

Delaware State Arts Council
Carvel State Office Building
820 North French Street
Wilmington, DE 19801
(302) 571-3540

Program/Award: Individual Artist Fellowship Program
Description: Fellowship program for individual creative artists.
Restrictions: Limited to Delaware residents. Recipients must reside in Delaware during the fellowship year; project year runs from October 1 through September 30.
Type of art: All Disciplines
$ given: $1,500 per fellowship for emerging professionals; $4,000 per fellowship for established professionals
Number of awards: 6–10 per year
Contact: John Gatti, Fellowship Coordinator
Application information: Write for guidelines and application materials. Must use official application form.
Deadline: March, with notification July 1 for most grants

Mid-Atlantic Arts Foundation
11 East Chase Street, Suite 2A
Baltimore, MD 21201
(301) 539-6656

Program/Award: Visual Arts Fellowships; Visual Arts Residency Program
Description: Fellowships and grants to individual artists in the Mid-Atlantic region and the U.S. Virgin Islands.
Restrictions: Limited to residents of Delaware, District of Columbia, Maryland, New Jersey, New York, Pennsylvania, Virginia, West Virginia, or the U.S. Virgin Islands.
Type of art: Visual Art

$ given: $5,000 per fellowship; $2,000 month per residency recipient, plus round-trip transportation between recipient's residence and host organization and $300 for slide documentation
Number of awards: Up to 20 fellowships per year; 25 residencies
Contact: Michelle Lamunière
Application information: Application forms and guidelines available in October of each year.

Pittsburgh Filmmakers
The Media Arts Center
205 Oakdale Avenue
P.O. Box 7467
Pittsburgh, PA 15213
(412) 681-5449

Program/Award: Mid-Atlantic Regional Arts Fellowship Program
Description: Fellowships for individual media artists.
Restrictions: Limited to residents of Delaware, District of Columbia, Maryland, New Jersey, Pennsylvania, or West Virginia. Applicants must have been residents of these states for at least 1 year prior to application.
Type of art: Film, Video, Media Art
$ given: Maximum of $5,000; Pennsylvania residents may apply for up to $7,000
Number of awards: N/A
Contact: Matthew Yokobosky, Fellowship Coordinator
Application information: Write or call for details.

District of Columbia

DC Commission on the Arts and Humanities
1111 E Street, NW
Suite B-500
Washington, DC 20004
(202) 724-5613

Program/Award: Individual Artist Fellowships

Description: 1-year fellowships to allow artists to pursue artistic goals and direction.

Restrictions: Limited to residents of the District of Columbia. Previous recipients may reapply, but grants are not awarded to the same artist more than 2 years in a row.

Type of art: Visual Art

$ given: $5,000 per fellowship

Number of awards: 20 annually

Contact: Barbara R. Nicholson, Executive Director; Jann Darsie, Staff Liaison for Visual Arts

Application information: Write for guidelines. Submit completed application form, résumé, slides, sample of original work, and SASE.

Deadline: N/A, with notification 8 months after deadline

Also see: Mid-Atlantic Arts Foundation/DELAWARE
Pittsburgh Filmmakers/DELAWARE

Florida

Florida Department of State
Division of Cultural Affairs
The Capitol
Tallahassee, FL 32399–0250
(904) 487-2980

Program/Award: Individual Artist Fellowships

Description: Fellowships for individual creative artists.

Restrictions: Applicants must be U.S. citizens who have been residents of Florida for at least one year, and who are age 18 or older. Recipients must maintain Florida residency during the grant period. Applicants must not be degree-seeking students either at the time of application or during the fellowship period. Recipients of Division fellowships during the past 5 years are not eligible.

Type of art: Dance, Visual Art, Media Art, Music Performance, Creative Writing, Theater

$ given: $5,000 per fellowship

Number of awards: N/A
Contact: Linda Downey, Chief, Bureau of Grant Services
Application information: Potential applicants urged to write for Guide to Grants.
Deadline: February 15, with notification in September

Also see: Appalshop/ALABAMA

Georgia

See: Appalshop/ALABAMA

Hawaii

See: Rocky Mountain Film Center/ARIZONA

Idaho

Idaho Commission on the Arts
304 West State Street
Boise, ID 83720
(208) 334-2119

Program/Award: Apprenticeship/Fellowship Grants
Description: Grants for individual Idaho artists to study with apprenticeship masters anywhere in the U.S.
Restrictions: Limited to Idaho residents age 18 and over.
Type of art: All Disciplines
$ given: Maximum of $3,500 per grant
Number of awards: 5–6 every 2 years
Contact: Gaetha Pace, Executive Director
Application information: Write or call the Commission for application forms.
Deadline: Spring, with notification within 2 months of deadline

Also see: Rocky Mountain Film Center/ARIZONA

Illinois

Arts Midwest
528 Hennepin Avenue, Suite 310
Minneapolis, MN 55403
(612) 341-0755

Program/Award: Visual Arts Fellowships
Description: Fellowships to individual regional visual artists.
Restrictions: Limited to residents of Illinois, Indiana, Iowa, Michigan, Minnesota, North Dakota, Ohio, South Dakota, and Wisconsin. Previous recipients may not reapply.
Type of art: Visual Art
$ given: $5,000 per fellowship
Number of awards: 20 per year
Contact: David Fraher, Executive Director
Application information: Write for application form and guidelines.
Deadline: March 29, with notification 4 months later

Center for New Television
11 East Hubbard
Chicago, Illinois 60611
(312) 565-1787

Program/Award: Regional Fellowship Program/Production Grants Program
Description: Funding through NEA/AFI for individual filmmakers and video makers to complete preproduction, shooting, editing, distribution, or some other definable stage of film or video.
Restrictions: Limited to residents of Illinois, Indiana, Michigan, and Ohio; must have been residents for at least 1 year. No student work. Applicant not eligible if applying for other NEA/AFI funding.
Type of art: Film, Video
$ given: Up to $5,000 per grant
Number of awards: N/A
Contact: N/A

Application information: Write for guidelines and forms.
Deadline: March 10

The Friends of Literature
c/o Mrs. Mabel A. Munger, President
300 North State Street, Apt. 4227
Chicago, IL 60610
(312) 321-1459

Program/Award: Annual Shakespeare Birthday Dinner and Awards Program
Description: Awards for best fiction, nonfiction, poetry, and civic contribution to Chicago-based writers.
Restrictions: Author must have had a connection with Chicago or the Chicago metropolitan area at some time during his or her life and/or career. Books must be published by a recognized trade publisher. Works should be of literary or scholarly merit; manuals, guides, reference works, and cookbooks are excluded.
Type of art: Fiction, Nonfiction, Poetry
$ given: $500 fiction award; $500 nonfiction award; $300 fiction/nonfiction award; $250 fiction/nonfiction award; $200 poetry award
Number of awards: 5 awards in 1990
Contact: Mrs. Mabel A. Munger, President
Application information: Submit 2 copies for review.
Deadline: January 15, with notification the first Saturday in May

Illinois Arts Council
State of Illinois Center
100 West Randolph Street, Suite 10-500
Chicago, IL 60601
(312) 814-6750

Program/Award: Artists Fellowships
Description: Nonmatching fellowships to individual Illinois artists who have demonstrated commitment to, and made outstanding contributions in, their fields.
Restrictions: Applicants must have established a minimum

6-month Illinois residency prior to application deadline. Limited to U.S. citizens and permanent resident aliens. Students not eligible.

Type of art: All Disciplines
$ given: Up to $6,000 per 6-month fellowship; most awards close to $1,000 each
Number of awards: 1,600 awards in fiscal year 1990
Contact: Illinois Arts Council, Program Offices
Application information: Write for application forms and documentation requirements.
Deadline: September 1, with notification in early November

Also see: Friends of American Writers/ARKANSAS

Indiana

Indiana Arts Commission
47 South Pennsylvania Street
Indianapolis, IN 46204
(317) 232-1268

Program/Award: Individual Artist Fellowships
Description: Funding for the creation or completion of a project, or for activities significant to the artist's professional growth.
Restrictions: Limited to Indiana residents.
Type of art: All Disciplines
$ given: Varies; usually maximum of 50 percent of project cost
Number of awards: N/A
Contact: Thomas B. Schorgl, Executive Director
Application information: Contact the Commission before applying. Ask for application guidelines for specific discipline.
Deadline: April 1

Also see: Arts Midwest/ILLINOIS
Center for New Television/ILLINOIS
Friends of American Writers/ARKANSAS

Iowa

Iowa State Arts Council
State Capitol Complex
Des Moines, IA 50319
(515) 281-4451

Program/Award: Creative Artists Grants
Description: Grants to support the cost of preparing works-in-progress for circulation, not for new work or general expenses. Artists are encouraged to apply through nonprofit organizations, though a significant amount of funding goes directly to individual artists.
Restrictions: Limited to Iowa residents.
Type of art: Creative Writing, Dance, Music Composition, Visual Art
$ given: $600 to $1,000 per grant
Number of awards: Approx. 25 per year to individuals
Contact: N/A
Application information: Write for application guidelines.
Deadline: January 10

Also see: Arts Midwest/ILLINOIS
Friends of American Writers/ARKANSAS

Kansas

Kansas Arts Commission
Jayhawk Towers, Suite 1004
700 Jackson
Topeka, KS 66603–3731
(913) 296-3335

Description: Funding programs for individuals and organizations; project grants for the coordination and development of the visual, performing, and literary arts in Kansas.
Restrictions: Limited to Kansas residents and organizations sponsoring arts projects in Kansas.
Type of art: Architecture, Visual Art, Creative Writing, Music, Theater, Dance, Media Art

$ given: For individuals, fellowships of $5,000; for organizations, grants ranging from $500 to $46,500, with most between $1,000 and $10,000
Number of awards: Varies; 3 fellowships in 1991, 4 in 1990; 137 awards to organizations in 1991
Contact: Dorothy L. Ilgen, Executive Director
Application information: Write for official application forms. Budget, résumé, etc., required with formal application.
Deadline: March 1 for grant requests of $500 or more

Also see: Friends of American Writers/ARKANSAS
Mid-America Arts Alliance/ARKANSAS

Kentucky

Kentucky Arts Council
Berry Hill
Louisville Road
Frankfort, KY 40601
(502) 564-3757

Program/Award: Al Smith Fellowships
Description: Fellowships for individual artists.
Restrictions: Limited to Kentucky residents.
Type of art: Music Composition, Dance, Media Art, Visual Art, Creative Writing
$ given: $5,000 per fellowship
Number of awards: 10 annually
Contact: Nancy Carpenter, Program Director
Application information: Write for application guidelines.

Also see: Appalshop/ALABAMA
Friends of American Writers/ARKANSAS

Louisiana

See: Appalshop/ALABAMA

Maine

See: Arts Extension Service/CONNECTICUT
Boston Film and Video Foundation/CONNECTICUT

Maryland

Maryland State Arts Council
15 West Mulberry Street
Baltimore, MD 21201
(301) 333-2778

Program/Award: Individual Artist Fellowships
Description: Grants to individual artists.
Restrictions: Limited to U.S. citizens who are Maryland residents, age 18 and over. Students not eligible.
Type of art: All Disciplines
$ given: $5,000 per fellowship
Number of awards: 16 annually
Contact: Ann McIntosh, Public Information Officer
Application information: Write for guidelines and application forms; publications available include bimonthly newsletter and incidental publications.
Deadline: Varies; usually late January

Maryland State Arts Council
15 West Mulberry Street
Baltimore, MD 21201
(301) 333-2778

Program/Award: Work-in-Progress Grants
Description: Grants to individual artists for the completion of works-in-progress.
Restrictions: Limited to U.S. citizens who are Maryland residents, age 18 and over. Students not eligible.
Type of art: All Disciplines
$ given: $200 to $2,000 per grant
Number of awards: 10 annually
Contact: Ann McIntosh, Public Information Officer

Application information: Write for guidelines and application forms; publications available include bimonthly newsletter and incidental publications.
Deadline: Varies; usually late January

Towson State University
College of Liberal Arts
Towson, MD 21204
(301) 321-2128

Program/Award: Towson State University Prize for Literature
Description: Annual prize for single book or book-length manuscript of fiction, poetry, drama, or imaginative nonfiction by a young Maryland writer.
Restrictions: Applicant must be 40 years of age or younger, and must have been a Maryland resident for at least 3 years immediately prior to the time of the award. Book must have been published within the 3 years prior to the award. Winning author must be willing to be present at the awards ceremony and to grant Towson State University the right to quote from the winning work in any publicity related to the prize.
Type of art: Creative Writing
$ given: $1,000 per prize (may be split if tie occurs)
Number of awards: 1 annually
Contact: Annette Chappell, Dean
Application information: Any individual, institution, group, or publisher may nominate 1 or more works for the prize. Submit 4 copies of the work by certified mail, bound if published or typewritten if manuscript. If manuscript, proof of acceptance by a publisher and proposed date of publication must be provided. A completed nomination form must accompany each entry; write to request the form.
Deadline: May 15, with notification in September

Also see: Mid-Atlantic Arts Foundation/DELAWARE
Pittsburgh Filmmakers/DELAWARE

Massachusetts

Artists Foundation
Massachusetts State Transportation Building
Eight Park Plaza
Boston, MA 02116
(617) 227-ARTS

Program/Award: The Massachusetts Artists Fellowship Program
Description: Fellowships for individual Massachusetts artists.
Restrictions: Limited to residents of Massachusetts over age 18
who are not in a degree-granting program.
Type of art: All Disciplines (19 categories)
$ given: $9,500 per fellowship; $500 per finalist award
Number of awards: 23 fellowships and 50 finalists in 1990
Contact: Rachel Blackman, Director of the Fellowship Program
Application information: Write for application forms. Support-
ing material required with formal application. Fellows must
wait 3 years before reapplying.
Deadline: First Monday in October or first Monday in March,
depending upon specific art category

Also see: Arts Extension Service/CONNECTICUT
Boston Film and Video Foundation/CONNECTICUT

Michigan

Michigan Council for the Arts
1200 Sixth Street
Detroit, MI 48226-2461
(313) 256-3731

Program/Award: Creative Artist Grants
Description: Grants to support works-in-progress or new works
by Michigan artists.
Restrictions: Limited to U.S. citizens who are Michigan residents.
Applicants must be working artists; students not eligible.
Type of art: Architecture, Dance, Media Art, Visual Art, Creative
Writing, and Book Art Composition

$ given: Maximum of $8,000 per grant
Number of awards: 70 per year
Contact: Craig Carver, Individual Artist Coordinator
Application information: Write for guidelines and deadline dates.

Also see: Arts Midwest/ILLINOIS
Center for New Television/ILLINOIS
Friends of American Writers/ARKANSAS

Minnesota

The Bush Foundation
E–900 First National Bank Building
St. Paul, MN 55101
(612) 227-0891

Program/Award: Bush Foundation Fellowships for Artists
Description: 6- to 18-month fellowships for full-time work in artists' chosen art forms. Allows artists to set aside a significant period of time to explore new directions or to accelerate work already in progress.
Restrictions: Limited to residents of Minnesota, North Dakota, and South Dakota. Applicants must be at least 25 years of age by filing deadline. (Writers must meet publication requirements.)
Type of art: Creative Writing, Visual Art, Media Art, Choreography, Music Composition
$ given: Maximum $24,000 per fellowship plus $6,240 for production and travel
Number of awards: Usually 15
Contact: Humphrey Doermann, President
Application information: Contact Foundation for application guidelines. Application form, sample of original work, project description, budget, SASE required for formal application. Former recipients may reapply 5 years after the conclusion of their fellowships.

Minnesota State Arts Board
432 Summit Avenue
St. Paul, MN 55102
(612) 297-2603

Program/Award: Artist Assistance Fellowship
Description: Annual fellowship funding for Minnesota artists.
Restrictions: Limited to U.S. citizens who are Minnesota residents, age 18 and over.
Type of art: Dance, Media Art, Music Performance, Theater, Creative Writing, Visual Art
$ given: $1,000 to $10,000 per fellowship
Number of awards: N/A
Contact: Karen Mueller, Program Associate
Application information: Write for up-to-date program information and necessary application forms.

Minnesota State Arts Board
432 Summit Avenue
St. Paul, MN 55102
(612) 297-2603

Program/Award: Sudden Opportunity Grant
Description: Ongoing funding for unforseen artistic opportunities.
Restrictions: Limited to U.S. citizens who are Minnesota residents, age 18 and over.
Type of art: Dance, Media Art, Music Performance, Theater, Creative Writing, Visual Art
$ given: $100 to $2,000 per grant
Number of awards: 6 per month
Contact: Karen Mueller, Program Associate
Application information: Write for up-to-date program information and necessary application forms.

Also see: Arts Midwest/ILLINOIS
Friends of American Writers/ARKANSAS

Mississippi

Mississippi Arts Commission
239 North Lamar Street
Suite 207
Jackson, MS 39201-1311
(601) 359-6030

Program/Award: Grants to Individuals
Description: Funding for individual Mississippi artists.
Restrictions: Limited to Mississippi residents.
Type of art: Theater, Dance, Music Performance, Creative Writing, Visual Art
$ given: Maximum of $7,500 per grant
Number of awards: N/A
Contact: Marian Bourdeaux, Program Administrator
Application information: Write for guidelines.
Deadline: February, with notification July 1

Missouri

See: Friends of American Writers/ARKANSAS
Mid-America Arts Alliance/ARKANSAS

Montana

Montana Arts Council
48 North Last Chance Gulch
Helena, MT 59620
(406) 443-4338

Program/Award: Individual Artist Fellowship
Description: Fellowships to individual Montana artists.
Restrictions: Limited to Montana residents, age 18 and over. Students not eligible. Individuals who received a fellowship within the last year not eligible.
Type of art: All Disciplines
$ given: $2,000 per fellowship
Number of awards: 10 annually

Contact: Julia A. Cook, Program Director
Application information: Write for guidelines.
Deadline: May 1, with notification in late June

Also see: Rocky Mountain Film Center/ARIZONA

Nebraska

See: Friends of American Writers/ARKANSAS
Mid-America Arts Alliance/ARKANSAS

Nevada

Nevada State Council on the Arts
329 Flint Street
Reno, NV 89501
(702) 789-0225

Program/Award: Artists-in-Residence Program
Description: Annual artist residency funding.
Restrictions: Limited to individuals who have been Nevada residents for at least 1 year prior to application.
Type of art: Visual Art, Creative Writing, Performing Art
$ given: $4,000 per artist residency
Number of awards: N/A
Contact: William Fox, Executive Director
Application information: Write the Council for up-to-date information on application policies.
Deadline: May 31, with notification by August 30

Nevada State Council on the Arts
329 Flint Street
Reno, NV 89501
(702) 789-0225

Program/Award: Special Projects Grants
Description: Direct assistance for artists' projects.
Restrictions: Limited to individuals who have been Nevada residents for at least 1 year prior to application.

Type of art: Visual Art, Creative Writing, Performing Art
$ given: Approx. $2,500 per grant
Number of awards: Approx. 10 annually
Contact: William Fox, Executive Director
Application information: Write the Council for up-to-date information on application policies.
Deadline: May 31, with notification by August 30

Also See: Rocky Mountain Film Center/ARIZONA

New Hampshire

New Hampshire State Council on the Arts
Phoenix Hall
40 North Main Street
Concord, NH 03301
(603) 271-2789

Program/Award: Artist Fellowships
Description: Fellowship funding for New Hampshire artists.
Restrictions: Limited to New Hampshire residents.
Type of art: All Disciplines
$ given: Average of $2,000 per fellowship
Number of awards: 7 annually
Contact: Susan Bonaiuto, Director
Application information: Write for guidelines and application forms.
Deadline: April 1

Also see: Arts Extension Service/CONNECTICUT
Boston Film and Video Foundation/CONNECTICUT

New Jersey

New Jersey State Council on the Arts
4 North Broad Street, CN 306
Trenton, NJ 08625
(609) 292-6130

Program/Award: Individual Fellowships

Description: Fellowship funding for New Jersey artists.
Restrictions: Limited to U.S. citizens who are New Jersey residents.
Type of art: Music, Dance, Visual Art, Creative Writing, Theater, Arts Education
$ given: Up to a maximum of $15,000 per fellowship
Number of awards: 368 fellowships awarded in 1989
Contact: Grants Office
Application information: Application requirements vary by discipline. All grants/fellowships are awarded on a fiscal year basis. The Council's fiscal year is July 1–June 30.
Deadline: Staggered according to art form, December through February

Also see: Mid-Atlantic Arts Foundation/DELAWARE
Pittsburgh Filmmakers/DELAWARE

New Mexico

New Mexico Arts Division
224 East Palace Avenue
Santa Fe, NM 87501
(505) 827-6490

Program/Award: Artist-in-Residence Program
Description: State residency program for artists.
Restrictions: Applicants must be New Mexico residents with at least 2 years of professional activity in their chosen disciplines.
Type of art: Architecture, Theater, Media Art, Music Composition, Dance, Visual Art, Creative Writing
$ given: $110 per day for short-term residency; $2,200 for 1 month residency; $1,390 per month for long-term residency
Number of awards: N/A
Contact: Joyce Hubert, Artist-in-Residence Coordinator
Application information: Write for guidelines and application forms.
Deadline: January

Also see: Dallas Museum of Art, Degolyer Fund/TEXAS
Rocky Mountain Film Center/ARIZONA

New York

The Center for Photography at Woodstock
59 Tinker Street
Woodstock, NY 12498
(914) 697-9957

Program/Award: The Photographers' Fund
Description: The Fund makes awards each year to regional photographers of vision and talent, selected by portfolio review by a panel of 3 noted national artists.
Restrictions: Limited to residents of 18 upstate New York counties (Albany, Columbia, Delaware, Dutchess, Fulton, Greene, Hamilton, Montgomery, Orange, Otsego, Rensselaer, Saratoga, Schenectady, Schoharie, Sullivan, Ulster, Warren, and Washington).
Type of art: Photography
$ given: $1,000 per award
Number of awards: 3 annually
Contact: Director
Application information: Write for details.

Checkerboard Foundation, Inc.
P.O. Box 222, Ansonia Station
New York, NY 10023

Program/Award: Checkerboard Foundation Video Awards
Description: Cash awards for video projects.
Restrictions: Limited to residents of New York State who have previously completed video work.
Type of art: Video
$ given: $5,000 to $10,000 per award
Number of awards: 2–4 per year
Contact: N/A
Application information: Write for guidelines.

PEN American Center
568 Broadway
New York, NY 10012
(212) 334-1660

Program/Award: PEN Writers Fund
Description: Emergency funds for writers.
Restrictions: Limited to residents of New York State.
Type of art: Creative Writing
$ given: $50 to $1,000, depending upon need
Number of awards: N/A
Contact: Christine Friedlander, PEN Writers Fund
Application information: Applications are accepted year-round. Reviews by committee approximately every 4–6 weeks.

Also see: Mid-Atlantic Arts Foundation/DELAWARE

North Carolina

North Carolina Arts Council
Department of Cultural Resources
Raleigh, NC 27611
(919) 733-7897 or 733-2821 or 733-2111

Program/Award: Artist Fellowships
Description: Annual fellowship funding for individual artists.
Restrictions: Limited to North Carolina residents who are professional artists.
Type of art: Music Composition, Dance, Media Art, Visual Art, Creative Writing
$ given: $5,000 per fellowship year
Number of awards: N/A
Contact: Jean A. Poston, Grants Officer
Application information: Write to request appropriate forms; applications will not be considered if not made on correct forms.
Deadline: Varies by discipline: Visual Art and Creative Writing, February 1; Performing Art, April 1

North Carolina Museum of History
109 East Jones Street
Raleigh, NC 27611
(919) 733-3894

Program/Award: Juried Exhibition of North Carolina Crafts
Description: Cash awards for winning craft items in triennial competition.
Restrictions: Limited to craftspersons who have been residents of North Carolina for at least 2 years.
Type of art: Crafts
$ given: $1,000 per award
Number of awards: 5 awards every 3 years
Contact: N/A
Application information: Write for guidelines.

Also see: Appalshop/ALABAMA

North Dakota

North Dakota Council on the Arts
Black Building, Suite 606
Fargo, ND 58102
(701) 237-8962

Program/Award: Artists Fellowships
Description: Fellowship funding to individual North Dakota artists.
Restrictions: Limited to U.S. citizens who are North Dakota residents.
Type of art: Dance, Media Art, Music Performance, Visual Art, Theater, Creative Writing
$ given: $5,000 per fellowship
Number of awards: N/A; fellowships given every 2 years, rotating among disciplines
Contact: Donna Evenson, Executive Director
Application information: Write for guidelines.

Also see: Arts Midwest/ILLINOIS
Bush Foundation/MINNESOTA
Friends of American Writers/ARKANSAS

Ohio

The Cleveland Museum of Art
11150 East Boulevard
Cleveland, OH 44106
(216) 421-7340

Program/Award: The May Show: Annual Exhibition by Artists and Craftsmen of the Western Reserve
Description: Cash awards and a purchase award for photography.
Restrictions: Work entered must be by artists who now live or work, or were born, in the following Ohio counties: Ashland, Ashtabula, Cuyahoga, Erie, Geauga, Huron, Lake, Lorain, Mahoning, Medina, Portage, Summit, or Trumbull.
Type of art: Visual Art
$ given: $1,000 per award
Number of awards: 5 annually, plus one purchase award for photography
Contact: Tom Hinson, Curator of Contemporary Art
Application information: Write for details.

Ohio Arts Council
727 East Main Street
Columbus, OH 43205
(614) 466-2613

Program/Award: Fellowships
Description: Fellowship funding for individual artists in various disciplines.
Restrictions: Limited to Ohio residents (of at least 6 months prior to application), age 18 and over. Applicants must not be enrolled in a degree- or certificate-granting program.
Type of art: All Disciplines
$ given: $4,500 or $9,000 per fellowship
Number of awards: 75–90 annually
Contact: Susan Dickson, Coordinator
Application information: Write for guidelines and application forms.
Deadline: January 15

Also see: Arts Midwest/ILLINOIS
Center for New Television/ILLINOIS
Friends of American Writers/ARKANSAS

Oklahoma

See: Dallas Museum of Art, Degolyer Fund/TEXAS
Friends of American Writers/ARKANSAS
Mid-America Arts Alliance/ARKANSAS

Oregon

Oregon Arts Commission
835 Summer Street, NE
Salem, OR 97301
(503) 378-3625

Program/Award: Individual Artist Fellowships
Description: Fellowship funding to individual Oregon artists.
Restrictions: Limited to Oregon residents.
Type of art: All Disciplines
$ given: $2,000 per fellowship
Number of awards: 15 annually (distributed across all disciplines)
Contact: Antonio Diez, Executive Director; Leslie Alexander, Assistant Director
Application information: Write for details.

Also see: Rocky Mountain Film Center/ARIZONA

Pennsylvania

Commonwealth of Pennsylvania Council on the Arts
216 Finance Building
Harrisburg, PA 17120
(717) 787-6883

Program/Award: Creative Artist Fellowships
Description: Annual fellowships for individual Pennsylvania artists.

Restrictions: Limited to Pennsylvania residents.
Type of art: Media Art, Visual Art, Music Composition, Dance, Creative Writing
$ given: Up to $5,000 per fellowship
Number of awards: N/A
Contact: Grants Officer
Application information: Write to request Guide to Fellowship Program from Council office. Forms and instructions for application are included in the guide.
Deadline: October 1, with notification mid-December

Also see: Mid-Atlantic Arts Foundation/DELAWARE
Pittsburgh Filmmakers/DELAWARE

Rhode Island

Rhode Island State Council on the Arts
95 Cedar Street, Suite 103
Providence, RI 02903–1034
(401) 277-3880

Program/Award: Artist Fellowships
Description: Fellowship funding for individual Rhode Island artists.
Restrictions: Applicants must have been residents of Rhode Island for at least 1 year prior to application. Applicants must be age 18 and over. Students not eligible. Applicants may not hold other fellowships concurrently with the Council's fellowship.
Type of art: Architecture, Music Composition, Dance, Media Art, Visual Art
$ given: $3,000 per fellowship
Number of awards: 10 annually
Contact: Edward Holgate, Director of Individual Artist Programs
Application information: Write for guidelines and deadline information.

Also see: Arts Extension Service/CONNECTICUT
Boston Film and Video Foundation/CONNECTICUT

South Carolina

South Carolina Arts Commission
1800 Gervais Street
Columbia, SC 29201
(803) 734-8696

Program/Award: Artist Fellowship Program
Description: Financial assistance to South Carolina artists who show significant potential; provides opportunities for more intensive individual development rather than short-term project support.
Restrictions: Applicants must be professional artists and legal residents of South Carolina. Full-time students, members and staff of the Commission are not eligible. Any artist who has ever received a SCAC Artist Fellowship may not reapply for 5 years.
Type of art: Visual Art, Crafts, Creative Writing, Music Performance
$ given: $5,000 per fellowship; funds must be expended within the fiscal year for which they are awarded
Number of awards: 6 annually; 2 for Visual Art, 1 for Crafts, 2 for Creative Writing, 1 for Music Performance
Contact: Ken May, Grants Coordinator
Application information: Applications must be made on proper forms and submitted with all required support materials.
Deadline: September 15, with notification in December

Also see: Appalshop/ALABAMA

South Dakota

South Dakota Arts Council
108 West 11th Street
Sioux Falls, SD 57102
(605) 339-6646

Program/Award: Project Grants
Description: Funding for individual artists' projects.
Restrictions: Limited to individuals who have been South Dakota residents for at least 2 years prior to application.

Type of art: All Disciplines
$ given: $100 to $15,000, based on project budget; grant funding must be matched 1 to 1
Number of awards: N/A
Contact: Dennis Holub, Executive Director
Application information: Write for guidelines and application forms.
Deadline: February 1

South Dakota Arts Council
108 West 11th Street
Sioux Falls, SD 57102
(605) 339-6646

Program/Award: Artist Fellowships
Description: Annual fellowship funding for South Dakota artists.
Restrictions: Limited to individuals who have been South Dakota residents for at least 2 years prior to application.
Type of art: All Disciplines
$ given: 2 fellowship funding categories; $5,000 and $1,000
Number of awards: 12 annually; 4 at $5,000 each, and 8 at $1,000 each
Contact: Dennis Holub, Executive Director
Application information: Write for guidelines and application forms.
Deadline: February 1

Also see: Arts Midwest/ILLINOIS
Bush Foundation/MINNESOTA
Friends of American Writers/ARKANSAS

Tennessee

Tennessee Arts Commission
320 Sixth Avenue North
Suite 100
Nashville, TN 37219
(615) 741-1701

Program/Award: Individual Artists Grants

Description: Funding for individual Tennessee artists.

Restrictions: Limited to individuals who have been residents of Tennessee for at least 6 months prior to application.

Type of art: All Disciplines

$ given: $2,500 to $5,000 per grant

Number of awards: 7–8 annually

Contact: Bennett Tarleton, Executive Director; Brenda Nunn, Director of Public Relations

Application information: Write for details.

Deadline: Varies by grant category; October–April

Also see: Appalshop/ALABAMA

Friends of American Writers/ARKANSAS

Texas

Dallas Museum of Art
1717 North Harwood
Dallas, TX 75201
(214) 922-1200

Program/Award: Clare Hart Degolyer Memorial Fund

Description: Funding to support younger, emerging visual artists who reside in the southwest U.S.

Restrictions: Limited to individuals, ages 15–25, who reside in Texas, Oklahoma, New Mexico, Arizona, or Colorado. Funds may not be used for college or art school tuition.

Type of art: Visual Art

$ given: Up to $1,500 per award

Number of awards: 2 awards in 1990

Contact: Curator of Contemporary Art

Application information: Applicants should send the following: (1) examples of their work, in the form of 5–10 labeled 35mm slides of high quality or videotape, each label including the artist's name, title of work, medium, and dimensions; (2) a current curriculum vitae, including birth date and full residency information for the past 3 years; (3) 2 letters of recommendation; (4) a short statement, accompanied by project

budget, of the purpose to which the award would be applied (travel, independent study, special project, etc.).
Deadline: March 1, with notification mid-May

Dallas Museum of Art
1717 North Harwood
Dallas, TX 75201
(214) 922-0220

Program/Award: Anne Giles Kimbrough Fund
Description: Direct grants to younger, emerging visual artists.
Restrictions: Applicants must be individuals, under age 30, who currently reside in Texas and have done so for the past 3 years. Funds may not be used for college or art school tuition.
Type of art: Visual Art
$ given: Up to $3,500 per grant
Number of awards: 5 awards in 1990
Contact: Curator of Contemporary Art
Application information: Write for guidelines.
Deadline: March 1, with notification mid-May

PEN American Center
568 Broadway
New York, NY 10012
(212) 334-1660

Program/Award: PEN/Southwest Houston Discovery Awards
Description: Cash awards to a poet and a fiction writer made to encourage and support new literary talent in the Houston area. Winners each give 4 public readings.
Restrictions: Applicants must have been residents of the Houston metropolitan area for at least 6 months and may not have had their work published in book form.
Type of art: Poetry, Fiction
$ given: $1,000 per award
Number of awards: 2 annually; 1 for poetry, 1 for fiction
Contact: PEN/Southwest, Department of English, University of Houston, Houston, TX 77004
Application information: Applicants should submit 15 pages of

poetry or 20–30 pages of prose (double-spaced) to the address in Houston. English or Spanish manuscripts are accepted. Manuscripts cannot be returned.
Deadline: January 15

The University of Texas at Austin
Office of the Vice President and Dean of Graduate Studies
Main Building 101
Austin, TX 78712
(512) 471-7213

Program/Award: Dobie-Paisano Project: Jesse H. Jones Writing Fellowship and Ralph A. Johnston Memorial Fellowship
Description: An opportunity for writers to live and work at Paisano, the late J. Frank Dobie's ranch near Austin. Recipients work without distractions in a setting of unique beauty and literary associations. Residencies are for 6 months each.
Restrictions: Limited to native Texans, current residents of Texas, or persons whose lives or work have been substantially identified with the state. No restrictions on subject matter. Term of residence is to be used for the creation of published works; visual artists may apply if their work will have accompanying text and the results are intended for publication.
Type of art: Creative Writing, Visual Art
$ given: $7,200 stipend per award plus residence at ranch
Number of awards: 2 awards: Jesse H. Jones Writing Fellowship and Ralph A. Johnston Memorial Fellowship
Contact: Dr. Audrey N. Slate
Application information: Write for guidelines and deadline information.

Also see: Mid-America Arts Alliance/ARKANSAS

Utah

Utah Arts Council
617 East South Temple Street
Salt Lake City, UT 84102
(801) 533-5757

Program/Award: Visual Artists Fellowships

Description: Annual fellowship funding for Utah artists.
Restrictions: Limited to Utah residents.
Type of art: Visual Art
$ given: $5,000 per fellowship
Number of awards: 2 annually
Contact: Dan Burke, Visual Arts Coordinator
Application information: Write for guidelines and application forms.
Deadline: December 31

Also see: Rocky Mountain Film Center/ARIZONA

Vermont

Stratton Arts Festival
Stratton Base Lodge
Stratton Mountain, VT 05155
(802) 297-2200

Program/Award: Elinor Janeway Fellowships; Juror's Award Program
Description: Fellowships to participating artists based on application describing project and quality of work on display; Juror's Awards presented for excellence of work on display.
Restrictions: Limited to residents of Vermont who are exhibitors at the annual Stratton Arts Festival.
Type of art: Visual Art
$ given: $1,000 per Janeway Fellowship; $500 per Juror's Award
Number of awards: 4 Janeway Fellowships; 6 Juror's Awards
Contact: Director, Stratton Arts Festival, P.O. Box 576, Stratton Mountain, VT 05155
Application information: Fellowship applications are available at the time of consignment.
Deadline: September 1, with notification September 15

Vermont Council on the Arts
136 State Street
Montpelier, VT 05602–3403
(802) 828-3291

Program/Award: Grants-in-Aid Fellowships

Description: Individual project awards.

Restrictions: Applicants must have been Vermont residents for at least 9 months prior to application.

Type of art: Visual Art, Film, Performing Arts (Dance, Theater, Music), Creative Writing

$ given: $2,000 per fellowship

Number of awards: 18 annually

Contact: Laura Hambleton, Public Information Officer; Geof Hewitt, Grants Coordinator

Application information: Write to request VCA Handbook, which contains application form. Artists will be required to submit samples of their work or to audition.

Deadline: March 1, with notification in July

Vermont Studio Center
P.O. Box 613
Johnson, VT 05656
(802) 635-2727

Program/Award: Vermont Studio Center Fellowship

Description: Scholarships to offset tuition.

Restrictions: Applicants must be age 25 and over.

Type of art: Visual Art, Creative Writing

$ given: Scholarships of 25–50 percent of tuition ($2,175 for 4-week summer session; $1,300 for winter session)

Number of awards: 72 annually

Contact: Jonathan T. Gregg, Co-Director

Application information: Write for guidelines.

Deadlines: November 30 and December 31

Also see: Arts Extension Service/CONNECTICUT
Boston Film and Video Foundation/CONNECTICUT

Virginia

Virginia Commission for the Arts
101 North 14th Street, 17th Floor
Richmond, VA 23219
(804) 225-3132

Program/Award: Individual Fellowships

Description: Fellowship funding for Virginia artists.
Restrictions: Limited to Virginia residents.
Type of art: Music Composition, Media Art, Visual Art, Creative
  Writing
$ given: $131,500 in fiscal year 1990
Number of awards: 26 in 1990
Contact: Regional Coordinator
Application information: Write for details.

Virginia Museum of Fine Arts
Office of Education and Outreach
2800 Grove Avenue
Richmond, VA 23221–2466
(804) 257-0824

Program/Award: Professional Fellowship Program; Student Fellowship Program
Description: Fellowships for undergraduate students, graduate
  students, and professionals in the visual arts, for additional
  education or experience in the arts.
Restrictions: Applicants must have lived in Virginia for at least
  5 of the last 10 years and must be a current Virginia resi-
  dent.
Type of art: Visual Art, Architecture, Media Art, Art History
$ given: $4,000 per Professional Fellowship; up to $4,000 per
  Student Fellowship. Payments usually made in installments
  over a 10-month period.
Number of awards: 23 in 1988–89
Contact: Susan F. Ferrell, Coordinator, Fellowships Program
Application information: Write to request application forms.
Deadline: Early March, with notification mid-May

Also see: Appalshop/ALABAMA
       Mid-Atlantic Arts Foundation/DELAWARE

Washington

Washington State Arts Commission
Mail Stop GH-11
Olympia, WA 98504
(206) 753-3860

Program/Award: Artists Fellowships
Description: Fellowship funding for Washington artists.
Restrictions: Limited to Washington residents.
Type of art: Music Composition, Dance, Media Art, Visual Art, Creative Writing
$ given: $5,000 per fellowship
Number of awards: 5 per year; categories rotate annually
Contact: Karen Gose
Application information: Write for application form and deadline information.
Deadline: Spring

Also see: Rocky Mountain Film Center/ARIZONA

West Virginia

West Virginia Department of Culture and History
The Cultural Center
Capitol Complex
Charlestown, WV 25305
(304) 348-0240

Description: Project grants to support the work of individual artists.
Restrictions: Limited to West Virginia residents.
Type of art: All Disciplines
$ given: Generally, the grant covers 50 percent of estimate project cost and requires a 1 to 1 match of funds
Number of awards: N/A
Contact: Lakin Ray Cook, Acting Director, Arts and Humanities Division
Application information: Write for application guidelines and forms.

Deadlines: April 1, August 1, February 1, with notification 90 days after deadlines

Also see: Mid-Atlantic Arts Foundation/DELAWARE
Pittsburgh Filmmakers/DELAWARE

Wisconsin

Council for Wisconsin Writers, Inc.
Box 55322
Madison, WI 53705
(608) 233-0531

Program/Award: Annual Writing Contest; Paulette Chandler Award
Description: The Annual Writing Contest presents awards for meritorious works in the following categories: (1) Book-length fiction; (2) Book-length nonfiction; (3) Juvenile book; (4) Nonfiction less than book length; (5) Book-length poetry collection; (6) Fiction less than book length; (7) Scholarly book; (8) Picture book for children; (9) Play; (10) Outdoor writing. The Chandler Award is given to the poet (in even-numbered years) and to the short story writer (in odd-numbered years) on the basis of ability and need.
Restrictions: Applicants must be Wisconsin authors meeting residency requirements of not less than 6 months, published within the current year.
Type of art: Creative Writing
$ given: $250 per first place award in each category for the Annual Writing Contest; $1,500 per Chandler Award
Number of awards: 10 Contest awards; 1 Chandler Award
Contact: Lynn Entine, President
Application information: Entry forms may be obtained from the address above.
Deadline: January 15

Wisconsin Arts Board
131 West Wilson Street, Suite 301
Madison, WI 53702
(608) 266-0190

Program/Award: Artist Fellowships
Description: Fellowships for individual Wisconsin artists.
Restrictions: Applicants must have been residents of Wisconsin
for at least 6 months prior to application and must remain
Wisconsin residents for the duration of the fellowship period.
Degree candidates not eligible.
Type of art: Music composition, Choreography, Creative Writ-
ing, Visual Art
$ given: $5,000 per fellowship
Number of awards: 8 per year; 3 in Visual Arts, 3 in Creative
Writing, and 2 in Composition (odd-numbered years) or Cho-
reography (even-numbered years)
Contact: Arley G. Curtz, Executive Director
Application information: Forms are available 45 days prior to
deadline. Applications reviewed by peer panelists. Board
makes final decision.
Deadline: September 15, with notification January 1

Wisconsin Arts Board
131 West Wilson Street, Suite 301
Madison, WI 53702
(608) 266-0190

Program/Award: Individual Project Grants
Description: Matching funds toward the completion of an indi-
vidual artist's work-in-progress.
Restrictions: Applicants must have been residents of Wisconsin
for at least 6 months prior to application and must remain
Wisconsin residents for the duration of the funded project.
Type of art: All Disciplines
$ given: Matching funds, up to 50 percent of project cost
Number of awards: N/A
Contact: Arley G. Curtz, Executive Director

Application information: Forms are available 45 days prior to deadline. Applications are reviewed by peer panelists. Board makes final decision.

Deadline: February 1, with notification after June 1

Also see: Arts Midwest/ILLINOIS
Friends of American Writers/ARKANSAS

Wyoming

Wyoming Council on the Arts
2320 Capitol Avenue
Cheyenne, WY 82002
(307) 777-7742

Program/Award: Individual Artist Assistance; Visual Arts—Individual Artist Fellowships; Literature—Individual Artist Fellowships

Description: Grants and fellowships to individual artists.

Restrictions: Limited to Wyoming residents.

Type of art: Visual Art, Creative Writing

$ given: Varies, $500 to $10,000. Matching funds may be required.

Number of awards: 130 grants per year (in all programs, to individual artists and to organizations)

Contact: Joy Thompson, Executive Director

Application information: Grant application forms available from Council.

Deadline: February 1, with notification in May

Also see: Rocky Mountain Film Center/ARIZONA

U.S. Territories

Virgin Islands Council on the Arts
Caravelle Arcade
Christiansted
St. Croix, USVI 00820
(809) 773-3075

Program/Award: Expanding Opportunities for Participation in the Arts

Description: Grants and technical assistance to individual artists, arts organizations, and art institutions in the U.S. Virgin Islands. Grants are considered on an individual need basis.

Restrictions: Applicants must be USVI residents, age 18 and over. No funding for capital improvements, erasing deficits, or scholarships.

Type of art: Architecture, Visual Art, Creative Writing, Music, Theater, Dance

$ given: Up to $5,000 per grant; varies by category. Matching funds (1 to 1) may be required.

Number of awards: Varies; 52 grants to individuals and organizations for fiscal year 1990

Contact: Stephen J. Bostic, Executive Director

Application information: Official application information available upon request.

Also see: Mid-Atlantic Arts Foundation/DELAWARE

III

*Fiscal Sponsorship
Monies,
by State*

Flow-Through Funding

The foundations in this section will not fund individuals directly. Instead, they give money only to organizations that are designated as charitable under section 501(c)(3) of the Internal Revenue Code. However, the individual artist can work through a nonprofit organization willing to act as a sponsor or parent organization. The monies awarded are paid directly to the nonprofit organization, which in turn pays the individual artist. Usually the nonprofit organization receives a fee of between 3 and 7 percent of monies raised. There is no upfront fee paid to the sponsor or parent organization; the 3 to 7 percent fee is customary, not obligatory.

How do you go about finding a nonprofit conduit? Check any local directory of nonprofit organizations available (your local library will usually have such directories in its collection, perhaps in a community services section). Contact local city-wide consortium-style organizations that operate in your area of interest such as art councils, federations, and so on. Speak to their directors and elicit their suggestions for possible sponsors. Talk to theater companies you have worked with, museums, dance companies, and so on. Any nonprofit organization you have ties to can become a conduit for flow-through funding.

Colorado

Colorado Council on the Arts and Humanities
770 Pennsylvania Street
Denver, CO 80203-3699
(303) 866-2617

Program/Award: Artists-in-Residence Program
Description: Matching grants to schools K–12 that sponsor professional artists in residence.
Restrictions: Limited to Colorado schools and artists.
Type of art: All Disciplines
$ given: N/A
Number of awards: N/A
Contact: Maryo G. Ewell, Director of Community Programs
Application information: Write for procedure information.
Deadline: February 15 for artists; March 1 for sponsors

Georgia

Georgia Council for the Arts
2082 East Exchange Plaza
Suite 100
Tucker, GA 30084
(404) 493-5780

Program/Award: Artist-Initiated Grants
Description: Funding for individual artists sponsored by nonprofit, tax-exempt organizations.
Restrictions: Artists must have been Georgia residents for at least 1 year prior to application. Sponsor organizations must be nonprofit, tax-exempt organizations incorporated in the State of Georgia.
Type of art: Architecture, Media Art, Music, Dance, Visual Art, Theater, Creative Writing
$ given: Maximum of $5,000 per grant
Number of awards: 25–30 per year
Contact: Frank Ratka, Director
Application information: Write for guidelines.
Deadline: May 1

Iowa

Iowa State Arts Council
State Capitol Complex
Des Moines, IA 50319
(515) 281-4451

Program/Award: Creative Artists Grants
Description: Grants intended to support the cost of preparing works-in-progress for circulation, not for new work or general expenses (i.e., not a fellowship). Artists are encouraged to work with nonprofit sponsoring organizations, but a significant amount of funding is given directly to individuals.
Restrictions: Limited to Iowa residents.
Type of art: Music Composition, Dance, Creative Writing, Visual Art
$ given: $600 to $1,000 per grant
Number of awards: 25 annually
Contact: N/A
Application information: Write for guidelines.
Deadline: Mid-January

Kentucky

Kentucky Arts Council
Berry Hill
Frankfort, KY 40601
(502) 564-3757

Description: Funding for arts sponsorship; grants to help sponsoring organizations reach and develop new audiences and strengthen themselves artistically or managerially.
Restrictions: Limited to nonprofit sponsoring organizations incorporated in the state of Kentucky. Out-of-state organizations may apply if they can show direct benefit to Kentucky audiences.
Type of art: All Disciplines
$ given: 50/50 matching funds; total varies according to project budget
Number of awards: 329 grants in fiscal year 1989

Contact: Roger L. Paige, Director
Application information: Write for guidelines.

Louisiana

Louisiana Division of the Arts
P.O. Box 44247
Baton Rouge, LA 70804
(504) 342-8180

Program/Award: Individual Artist Projects/Fiscal Agents
Description: Funding for individual artists sponsored by non-profit organizations acting as fiscal agents.
Restrictions: Limited to Louisiana artists and sponsoring organizations. An organization may sponsor up to 3 projects. A reasonable relationship should exist between the project type and the primary purpose of the fiscal agent; however, the project must clearly be an individual artist's project and not an extension of the fiscal agent's programming.
Type of art: All Disciplines
$ given: N/A
Number of awards: N/A
Contact: Derek E. Gordon, Executive Director
Application information: Call or write for guidelines and application form.
Deadline: Early March

Maine

Maine Arts Commission
State House Station 25
Augusta, ME 04333
(207) 289-2724

Program/Award: Artist-in-Residence Program
Description: Funding to assist sponsoring organizations in hosting artist residencies, ranging in duration from 10 days to 1 year.
Restrictions: Individual applicants must be professional artists, sponsored by organizations. Maine residents are given priority funding.

Type of art: Architecture, Visual Art, Dance, Media Art, Theater, Creative Writing
$ given: N/A
Number of awards: N/A
Contact: N/A
Application information: Write for appropriate forms.
Deadline: Early February

Maine Arts Commission
State House Station 25
Augusta, ME 04333
(207) 289-2724

Program/Award: Maine Touring Artists Program
Description: Funding to assist sponsored artists in touring the state.
Restrictions: Artists must be Maine residents and professionals of high caliber, sponsored by organizations. Artists/sponsors are responsible for finding their own bookings throughout Maine. Performing artists must participate in 2 state-funded activities during the year, 1 of which must be a public performance.
Type of art: All Disciplines
$ given: Varies; sponsoring organization must supply a minimum of two thirds of the artist's fee
Number of awards: N/A
Contact: N/A
Application information: Write for guidelines and deadline dates.

Massachusetts

Massachusetts Council on the Arts and Humanities
The Little Building
80 Boylston Street, 10th Floor
Boston, MA 02116
(617) 727-3668

Program/Award: Contemporary Arts funding programs to support artists and sponsoring organizations with new work. Programs include: Art Exchange, Mass Productions, New Works, Massachusetts Art in Public Places, Massachusetts Artists Fellowship Program.

Restrictions: Artists must apply through sponsoring, nonprofit organizations.

Type of art: All Disciplines

$ given: Varies widely according to program; $19.44 million in total budget; many programs require matching funds

Number of awards: Approx. 1,200 awards each year for all programs combined

Contact: Anne Hawley, Executive Director

Application information: Write to request the MCAH program guidelines and deadline information.

Missouri

Missouri Arts Council
111 North 7th Street, Suite 105
St. Louis, MO 63101
(314) 444-6845

Program/Award: Creative Artists Project

Description: Funding for individual artists who apply through sponsoring organizations.

Restrictions: Applicants must be U.S. citizens who have been residents of Missouri for at least 2 years prior to application. Students and performing artists not eligible.

Type of art: Architecture, Music Composition, Choreography, Media Art, Visual Art, Creative Writing

$ given: Matching funds on 1 to 1 basis with sponsoring organization; maximum match of $5,000

Number of awards: N/A

Contact: Teresa Goettsch, Program Administrator

Application information: Write for guidelines and deadline dates.

Nebraska

Nebraska Arts Council
1313 Farnam-on-the-Mall
Omaha, NE 68102-1873
(402) 554-2122

Program/Award: Artists-in-Schools/Communities
Description: Funding for professional artists in school/community residencies.
Restrictions: Applicants must be practicing artists of professional excellence, sponsored by a nonprofit organization in Nebraska. Students not eligible. Artists must make application for eligibility, but eligibility does not guarantee employment. Eligible artists may be employed by organizations that receive grants.
Type of art: All Disciplines
$ given: $650 per 1-week residency (includes travel expenses); $3,250 per 9-week residency (includes travel expenses)
Number of awards: More than 200 per year
Contact: Arts Education Coordinator
Application information: Write to be placed on mailing list; application forms and instructions mailed after December 1.
Deadline: February 1

Nebraska Arts Council
1313 Farnam-on-the-Mall
Omaho, NE 68102–1873
(402) 554-2122

Program/Award: Nebraska Touring Program
Description: Funding to nonprofit organizations that utilize professional artists in statewide touring programs.
Restrictions: Applicants must be Nebraska residents sponsored by nonprofit organizations.
Type of art: Theater, Dance, Media Art, Music, Visual Art
$ given: Approximately 40 percent of funded artists' fees
Number of awards: Approximately 110 per year
Contact: Douglas D. Elliot, Associate Director of Programs

Application information: Write for guidelines, application forms, and deadline dates.

New York

New York Council on the Arts
915 Broadway
New York, NY 10010
(212) 614-2904

Program/Award: Individual Artist Program
Description: Funding for project support in the creation of new works.
Restrictions: Applicant must be sponsored by nonprofit organization.
Type of art: Media Art, Music Composition, Theater, Visual Art
$ given: $1,599,987 in fiscal year 1990
Number of awards: 146 in 1990
Contact: Individual Artist Program
Application information: Write for guidelines and application forms.
Deadline: March 1

Ohio

Ohio Arts Council
727 East Main Street
Columbus, OH 43205–1796
(614) 466-2613

Program/Award: Dance Support Program
Description: Funding for professional dance companies; funding for projects that support new and innovative choreography, especially works by Ohio choreographers; funding for performance projects conceived by professional artists sponsored by nonprofit organizations.
Restrictions: Sponsoring organizations must be based in Ohio; preference for funding individual Ohio choreographers' and performance artists' projects.
Type of art: Dance

$ given: $5,586 average grant
Number of awards: 21 awards in fiscal year 1989
Contact: Jackie Calderone, Dance Program Coordinator
Application information: Organization must include these materials with application form: budget breakout, résumés and job descriptions of professional and key personnel, description of selection/audition process, detailed performance schedule, list of company's active repertoire, promotional material, media reviews, audience attendance figures, list of board members, outline of guest artists' residence activities, outline of workshop activities.
Deadline: December 1 for notice of intent to apply (via letter, phone call, visit); April 1 for submission of all necessary materials

Oklahoma

State Arts Council of Oklahoma
Jim Thorpe Building, Room 640
Oklahoma City, OK 73105
(405) 521-2931

Program/Award: Artist-in-Residence Program
Description: Funding for nonprofit organizations that sponsor individual artist residencies, which may range in duration from 1 week to 1 semester.
Restrictions: Sponsors must be nonprofit, nonreligious organizations, such as schools, civic groups, and local government agencies, located in Oklahoma.
Type of art: Theater, Dance, Music Performance, Visual Arts, Creative Writing
$ given: N/A; partial funding for artists' fees
Number of awards: N/A
Contact: Betty Price, Executive Director
Application information: Write for guidelines and forms.
Deadlines: April 1 for residencies between July 1 and December 31; October 1 for residencies between January 1 and June 30; 60 days prior to residency dates for new sites

Not Geographically Restricted

Foundation for Independent Video and Film, Inc.
625 Broadway, 9th Floor
New York, NY 10012
(212) 473-3400

Program/Award: Donor-Advised Film Fund
Description: Funding for the following film/video awards: Marjorie Benton Peace Film Award for completed film or video that best promotes understanding of peace issues; Post-Production Grant for work-in-progress that is substantially completed; Beldon Fund Grants for production, editing, completion, or distribution of works dealing with environmental issues.
Restrictions: Applicants must be affiliated with nonprofit organizations. Institutional projects for internal or promotional use, productions of public television stations, and student projects are not eligible.
Type of art: Film, Video
$ given: $5,000 per Benton Award; $10,000 per Post-Production Grant; $20,000 total for all Beldon Fund Grants
Number of awards: Minimum of 3 per year
Contact: N/A
Application information: Write for guidelines and application forms.
Deadline: Early July

Meet the Composer, Inc.
2112 Broadway, Suite 505
New York, NY 10023
(212) 787-3601

Program/Award: Composers Performance Fund
Description: Funding toward composers' fees when presenting organizations invite composers for events featuring their music and personal participation.
Restrictions: All composers and all not-for-profit organizations are eligible.

Type of art: Music Composition
$ given: $150 to $1,000 per grant; sponsor organization bears cost of program and publicity
Number of awards: 2,200 grants for the year 1989–90
Contact: John Duffy, President
Application information: Formal application forms are available from the address above. Evaluation is based on quality of program, fiscal credibility of presentor, participation of composer, audience size, composer résumé, and geographic spread.
Deadlines: May 1 for events between July 1 and September 30; August 1 for events between October 1 and February 15; December 1 for events between February 16 and June 30

IV

Federal Funding Sources

National Endowment for the Arts
1100 Pennsylvania Avenue, NW
Washington, DC 20506

Promotion of the Arts—Design Arts Program
(202) 682-5437

Description: Grants for design projects that have the potential for producing results of exceptional merit and national or regional significance. Categories include: Design Advancement (for theory, research, education); USA Fellowships (independent study for designers in mid-career); and Distinguished Designer Fellowships (for outstanding contributions over the course of a career).

Restrictions: N/A

Type of art: Architecture, Landscape Architecture, Environmental Design, Fashion Design, Industrial Design, Interior Design, Urban Design

$ given: Up to $15,000 per Design Advancement grant to individual; up to $20,000 per USA Fellowship and Distinguished Designer Fellowship

Number of awards: 148 in all design categories in fiscal year 1988

Contact: Randolph McAusland, Director, Design Arts Program

Application information: Write for brochure and deadline dates.

Promotion of the Arts—Media Arts:
Film/Radio/Television
(202) 682-5452

Description: Grants in support of projects designed to assist individuals and groups in producing films, radio, and video of high aesthetic quality, and to exhibit and disseminate media arts. Funding also provided through the American Film Institute.

Restrictions: Funding limited to individual artists, nonprofit organizations, and local and state government agencies.

Type of art: Film, Video, Media Art

$ given: Grants range from $2,500 to $500,000

Number of awards: N/A

Contact: Director, Media Arts Program

Application information: Write for guidelines and deadline dates.

Promotion of the Arts—Dance
(202) 682-5435

Program/Award: Choreographers' Fellowships

Description: Financial assistance for individual choreographer's artistic growth. Not a commission program. Work done during the grant period need not culminate in a performance. Fellowship funds can be used for any project or activity which will aid a choreographer's creative development, including travel for dance-related purposes.

Restrictions: Individual choreographers eligible; choreographers who are artistic directors of professional companies funded by the NEA Dance Program are ineligible.

Type of art: Choreography

$ given: Fellowships at levels of $7,500, $10,000, and, in rare instances, $15,000

Number of awards: 97 fellowships in fiscal year 1988

Contact: Director, Dance Program

Application information: Write to request guidelines and application procedures. Applicants should not specify level of funding requested; panel will decide. Applicants should request 1-year fellowships, but panel may recommend a limited number of 3-year fellowships.

Deadline: Early December, with notification in October

Program/Award: Dance/Film/Video

Description: Assistance to organizations and individuals who use film or video creatively to preserve, enhance, and expand the art of dance. Grants are awarded primarily for projects in which dance takes precedence over the film or video art form.

Restrictions: Open to tax-exempt organizations in continuous operation for at least 3 years, with a professional staff, highest quality dancers, and proven fund-raising ability. Grants generally available only for projects involving filmmakers and video makers who have had prior experience working with dance.

Type of art: Dance, Film, Video

$ given: $5,000 to $20,000 per grant to organization; up to $15,000 per grant to individual (most awards substantially less)

Number of awards: 13 in fiscal year 1988

Contact: Director, Dance Program

Application information: Write for guidelines and application procedures.

Deadline: Mid-November, with notification the following October

Promotion of the Arts—Music
(202) 682-5445

Program/Award: Composers Program

Description: Composers Fellowships/Collaborative Fellowships to encourage the creation of new compositions and the completion of works-in-progress, and generally to assist professional development.

Restrictions: Available to composers and collaborators, such as librettists, video artists, filmmakers, poets, and choreographers. Grants are also available to music performing organizations to enable them to engage composers-in-residence.

Type of art: Music Composition

$ given: Up to $25,000 per Composer Fellowship; up to $35,000 per Collaborative Fellowship

Number of awards: N/A
Contact: Music Program
Application information: Write for guidelines, forms, and deadline dates.

Program/Award: Jazz
Description: Grants to individual professional jazz performers for support of rehearsals, performances, and the preparation of audio and video demo tapes and related expenses. Grants to professional jazz composers for creation of new works, completion of works-in-progress, and reproduction of scores or parts of completed works. Fellowships for distinguished jazz masters. Support to individuals for innovative and examplary special projects of national or regional significance.
Restrictions: N/A
Type of art: Music Performance, Music Composition
$ given: $3,000 to $7,500 per individual grant for performers and composers; up to $20,000 per Jazz Masters fellowship; $5,000 to $10,000 per project assistance grant
Number of awards: N/A
Contact: Music Program
Application information: Write for guidelines, forms, and deadline dates.

Program/Award: Music Recording
Description: Matching grants for nonprofit organizations and solo and duo performers for the recording and distribution of American music.
Restrictions: N/A
Type of art: Music Performance
$ given: $5,000 to $20,000 per grant; must be matched on 1 to 1 basis
Number of awards: N/A
Contact: Music Program
Application information: Write for guidelines, forms, and deadline dates.

Program/Award: Solo Recitalists
Description: Fellowships to individuals of outstanding talent

with the potential for major careers as solo recitalists. Program operates on a 2-year cycle: fiscal year 1991 fellowships to vocalists and keyboard instrumentalists; fiscal year 1992 fellowships to all other instrumentalists.

Restrictions: N/A
Type of art: Music Performance—Vocal/Instrumental
$ given: $7,500 to $15,000 per fellowship
Number of awards: 203
Contact: Music Program
Application information: Write for guidelines, forms, and deadline dates.

Promotion of the Arts—Opera and Musical Theater
(202) 682-5447

Description: Funding to support excellence in the performance and creation of professional opera and musical theater throughout the nation.
Restrictions: Available to nonprofit organizations, as well as state and local government agencies.
Type of art: Opera, Musical Theater
$ given: $5,000 to $350,000 per grant
Number of awards: Varies; in 1990, a total of 199 grants to individuals and organizations.
Contact: Director, Opera/Musical Theater Program
Application information: Write for guidelines, forms, and deadline dates.

Promotion of the Arts—Theater
(202) 682-5425

Program/Award: Director Fellows
Description: Grants to individual stage directors of exceptional talent in their early career development. Opportunities may include working with one or more professional theaters, assisting and observing the work of distinguished directors, or

working on independent projects. This program is administered through Theatre Communications Group, (212) 697-5230.

Restrictions: N/A
Type of art: Theater
$ given: $22,000 in awards; $18,000 in grants; $90,000 in fellowships
Number of awards: 2 awards, 3 grants, 6 fellowships
Contact: Grants Office, Theater, or Theatre Communications Group
Application information: Write for guidelines and deadline dates.

Program/Award: Fellowships for Playwrights
Description: Fellowships to assist playwrights of exceptional talent to set aside time for writing, research, or travel, and to advance their careers.
Restrictions: N/A
Type of art: Playwriting
$ given: Up to $17,500 per fellowship; plus $2,500 to defray costs of residency at a professional theater of the playwright's choice. Use of residency funds restricted to travel and living expenses associated with residency at host theater. One-year awards made in total amounts up to $20,000; a limited number of 2-year awards made in amounts up to $37,500.
Number of awards: N/A
Contact: Grants Office, Theater
Application information: Write for guidelines, forms, and deadlines dates.

Program/Award: Fellowships for Mimes and Solo Performance Artists
Description: Grants to exceptionally talented professional individual artists working independently of companies and exploring new styles and forms of theater, including puppetry. Financial assistance for activities that contribute to an individual's artistic growth.
Restrictions: N/A
Type of art: Performance Art
$ given: $5,000 to $12,500 per grant

Number of awards: N/A
Contact: Grants Office, Theater
Application information: Write for guidelines, forms, and deadline dates.

Program/Award: Distinguished Artist Fellowships in Theater
Description: Fellowships for artists in theater who are making extraordinary contributions to the art form. Four one-time fellowships awarded in recognition of an artist's overall contribution and record of accomplishment in the not-for-profit theater.
Restrictions: N/A
Type of art: Theater
$ given: N/A
Number of awards: 4 annually
Contact: Grants Office, Theater
Application information: Write for guidelines, forms, and deadline dates.

Program/Award: Stage Designer Fellows
Description: Grants to encourage the development of early career stage designers in the not-for-profit theater.
Restrictions: N/A
Type of art: Theater
$ given: N/A
Number of awards: N/A
Contact: Grants Office, Theater
Application information: Write for guidelines, forms, and deadline dates.

Promotion of the Arts—Literature
(202) 682-5451

Description: Fellowships to published creative writers and translators of exceptional talent, in two categories: (1) Fellowships for Creative Writers: Fiction, Poetry, and Creative Nonfiction; (2) Fellowships for Translators.
Restrictions: Applicants must be U.S. citizens or permanent residents who have published work.

Type of art: Creative Writing
$ given: $20,000 per Creative Writer fellowship; $10,000 to $20,000 per Translator fellowship, depending upon length and scope of project
Number of awards: N/A
Contact: Program Administrator, Literature Program
Application information: Write for guidelines, forms, and deadline dates.

Promotion of the Arts—Visual Arts
(202) 682-5448

Description: Grants to assist painters, sculptors, craftsmen, photographers, and printmakers; fund to support institutions devoted to the development of the visual arts in America.
Restrictions: Funding available to individual U.S. citizens, nonprofit organizations, and state and local government agencies.
Type of art: Painting, Sculpture, Crafts, Photography, Printmaking
$ given: Grants range from $1,000 to $50,000 each
Number of awards: N/A
Contact: Director, Visual Arts Program
Application information: Write for guidelines, forms, and deadline dates.

Program/Award: Visual Artists Fellowships
Description: Grants to encourage the creative development of professional artists, enabling them to pursue their work.
Restrictions: Applicants must be U.S. citizens or permanent residents. Students not eligible. Recipients of $5,000 fellowships may reapply each funding cycle; recipients of $20,000 fellowships may reapply after two 2-year cycles.
Type of art: Painting, New Genres (conceptual, performance, video), and Works on Paper (printmaking, drawing) alternate annually with Crafts, Photography, and Sculpture
$ given: Fellowships of either $5,000 or $20,000 each
Number of awards: N/A
Contact: Michael Faubion, Acting Director; Silvio Lim, Program Specialist/Fellowships

Application information: Write for guidelines, forms, and deadlines dates.

Promotion of the Arts—Folk Arts
(202) 682-5449

Description: Funding to assist, foster, and make publicly available the diverse traditional American folk arts.

Restrictions: Funds available to individuals, nonprofit organizations, and state and local government agencies.

Type of art: Folk Arts

$ given: Grants range from $1,000 to $50,000 each

Number of awards: N/A

Contact: Director, Folk Arts Program

Application information: Write for guidelines, forms, and deadline dates.

Inter-Arts Program
(202) 682-5444

Description: Funding in several categories, mostly for organizations, artist communities, and service organizations, but also for projects that result in the creation of original work that challenges the traditional arts disciplines.

Restrictions: Open to artists' projects involving innovative work, and to collaborations of artists of different disciplines or new technologies.

Type of art: Multidisciplinary

$ given: $5,000 to $15,000 (with a few exceeding $35,000) for each artist's project; grants require matching funds on a 1 to 1 basis

Number of awards: N/A

Contact: Joel Snyder, Acting Director, Inter-Arts Program

Application information: Write for guidelines and deadline dates.

United States–Japan Artist Exchange Fellowship Program
(202) 682-5562

Description: Under an exchange agreement between governments, 5 fellowships for 6 consecutive months each are awarded annually to Americans in the creative and performing arts in the hope that exposure to Japan will have an impact on their creative work. Five Japanese artists receive fellowships to the U.S.

Restrictions: Limited to U.S. citizens and permanent residents who have not been residents of Japan for more than 2 months and who have not received grants of a similar nature. Students, scholars, and art critics not eligible.

Type of art: Design, Dance, Visual Art, Creative Writing, Theater, Music, Media Art

$ given: 400,000 yen per month (for 6 months) plus round-trip transportation

Number of awards: 5 annually

Contact: Beverly Kratochvil, Program Officer, International Activities

Application information: Write for guidelines and application forms.

Deadlines: Vary according to specific arts discipline

Arts and Artifacts Indemnity
(202) 682-5442

Description: Provides for indemnification against loss or damage of eligible works, artifacts, and objects when borrowed from abroad on exhibition in the U.S., and when borrowed from the U.S. for exhibition abroad, in cases of exchange exhibitions with foreign countries.

Restrictions: Funding available to individuals, nonprofit organizations, and state and local government agencies.

Type of art: Physical Art Objects

$ given: Insurance ranging in coverage from $500,000 to $50 million per policy

Number of awards: N/A
Contact: Indemnity Administrator, Museums Program
Application information: Write for guidelines.

Promotion of the Arts—Arts Administration Fellows Program
(202) 682-5786

Description: Limited number of 13-week fellowships in an office of the NEA, to give professionals and students in arts administration and related fields a working view of the agency's operations. Time is provided for participants to attend seminars on management and fund-raising. Activities provide detailed knowledge of NEA's programs, including policy development, grantmaking procedures, and internal administration. Participants selected on competitive basis according to prior professional experience.
Restrictions: N/A
Type of art: Arts Administration
$ given: $4,000 stipend per 13-week fellowship plus round-trip travel to Washington, DC
Number of awards: 46 fellowships in fiscal year 1987
Contact: Arts Administration Fellows Program Coordinator
Application information: Write for application forms and detailed information.
Deadline: 5 months prior to start of session; 3 sessions per year

National Endowment for the Humanities
1100 Pennsylvania Avenue, NW
Washington, DC 20506

Promotion of the Humanities—Younger Scholars
(202) 786-0273

Description: Funding to support noncredit humanities projects during the summer, initiated and conducted by young persons. Grants awarded for research, education, film, and community projects in one or more of the fields included in the humanities: history, philosophy, language, linguistics, literature, archaeology, jurisprudence, art history, and criticism, and the humanistic social sciences.

Restrictions: Limited to individuals age 30 or younger.
Type of art: Film, Literature
$ given: Grants range from $1,800 to $2,200
Number of awards: N/A
Contact: Director, Office of Youth Programs, Room 426
Application information: Write for guidelines, forms, and deadline dates.

Promotion of the Humanities—Summer Stipends (202) 786-0466

Description: Funding to provide time to scholars, writers, and other interpreters of the humanities for uninterrupted study and research.
Restrictions: Applicants must have produced or demonstrated promise of producing significant contributions to humanistic knowledge.
Type of art: Literature
$ given: $3,000 per grant
Number of awards: N/A
Contact: Program Officer for Summer Stipends, Division of Fellowships and Seminars
Application information: Write for guidelines, forms, and deadline dates.

General Services Administration
18th and F Streets, NW
Washington, DC 20405
(202) 501-3950

Art-in-Architecture Program

Description: Funding for commissioned art work on the sites of federal buildings as part of the overall building design.

Restrictions: Artists commissioned must be U.S. citizens.

Type of art: Visual Art

$ given: N/A

Number of awards: 10 works commissioned and 2 installed in 1990

Contact: Director

Application information: Write to General Services Administration (PGA) for fact sheet. Formal application requires submission of slides and résumé.

Deadline: Ongoing funding; deadlines dependent upon building project dates

V

Sample Proposals

THE INGRAM MERRILL FOUNDATION

POST OFFICE BOX 202, VILLAGE STATION, NEW YORK CITY 10014

APPLICATION FOR AWARD OR GRANT

Must be typewritten

Name _____ Anne _____ Elizabeth _____ Josephs _____
      First   *Middle name or initial*   *Last name*

Address ___ 132 West 28th Street, New York, NY 10010 _____

Telephone no. ___ (212) 555-1379 _____

I. PERSONAL HISTORY

Present occupation ___ Design Consultant _____

Place of birth ___ Yonkers, New York ___ Date of birth ___ 4/27/49 _____

Are you an American citizen? __ Yes __   If you are a naturalized citizen
give date and place of naturalization.

_____

If you are not an American citizen, give country of which you are a citizen,
subject, or national.

_____

Are you now, or will you be at any time falling within the period of your project, a
representative, agent, or employee of any foreign nation or political subdivision,
or political party thereof? If so, give details.

___ No _____

Number of dependents, other than yourself. ___ None _____

What is your estimated income from other sources in the year or years in which you
will be working on your project? A detailed answer is necessary.

Consultant in decorative arts and textiles - $20,000

Teaching - $2,000

II. ACADEMIC AND OCCUPATIONAL BACKGROUND

Summarize your academic background, listing colleges, universities, or other institutions of learning attended, with degrees, diplomas, and certificates held.

Syracuse University, School of Visual and Performing Arts

— B.F.A. Degree 1970

Summarize your occupational background, indicating employer, position held, and dates of tenure.

Lawson Houston, Ltd.   Design Consultant and Writer
Aug. 1986-present

Cohama Riverdale   Director of Design
Oct. 1980-July 1986

Parsons School of Design   Part-time Instructor
Sept. 1983-present

Waverly Fabrics div./Schumacher   Design Director
Dec. 1974-Oct. 1980

List all fellowships, grants, and scholarships you have received, giving full details of each, including name of grantor, amount of stipend, and studies or work carried on thereunder.

None

List your publications, giving title, publisher, and date of publication of each. Submit copies of all of this work with your application, unless it is totally irrelevant to the present project. One copy of each is sufficient. Painters and sculptors should supply representative slides of their work. All applicants must enclose a stamped, self-addressed envelope for the return of materials submitted.

III. DESCRIPTION OF PROJECT

Concise statement of project ___We are writing a book on historical interiors and residences (18th–early 20th century) that combines both Eastern and Western styles of design, becoming hybrids of both worlds. It would be of significant interest to design students, professionals, and decorative arts historians.___

A more detailed statement of your project and of your plans for work may be attached.

When do you wish to begin your project? ___January 1991___

Give your best estimate of time required for its completion. ___1 year___

Give an estimate of the sum which you feel you will require from this Foundation in order to carry out your project.

___$7,500___

When do you desire payment? Keep in mind that funds are available once a year only; approximately the first of the year. Your application must be received by the 15th of August for consideration in that year.

___January 1991___

Have you applied elsewhere for a fellowship, grant, or scholarship for the same project or for another project for the same period of time? If so, give details.

John Simon Guggenheim Memorial Foundation, Rockefeller

Foundation Humanities Fellowships, Marguerite Ever Wilbur

Foundation, Graham Foundation for Advanced Study in the

Fine Arts

237

IV. REFERENCES

Give names of three or more persons who can supply further information with regard to your qualifications, and (if your project is of a scholarly nature) who can give expert opinion concerning the value of this project as a contribution to knowledge; ask them to write on your behalf as soon as you submit your application.

Mr. David Smith	Curator, Cooper-Hewitt Museum
Mr. Samuel Foley	Retired (1986) Dean of Continuing Education Parsons School of Design, Consult. to New York School of Interior Design
Ms. Katherine Johns	Editor, Simon & Schuster
Ms. Sarah Pickens	Professor, University of California at Davis
Mr. David Levy	Vice-President, Waverly/Schumacher

(If in any of the foregoing items sufficient space is not allowed for a full and complete answer, it is requested that the information called for be stated in a separate paper securely attached to this application form. Each such separate paper should be signed and dated by the applicant. The application, which must be typed, should be mailed to The Ingram Merrill Foundation, Post Office Box 202, Village Station, New York, NY 10014.)

Anne Josephe
Signature

September 12, 1990
Date

NOTE: Any false, misleading, or incomplete answer or statement in any of the items above shall be ground for the immediate termination of any scholarship or fellowship that may be awarded on this application.

Please note that the foundation does not grant personal interviews; applications are to be submitted by mail only.

| Individual Grant Application | Visual Arts Program |
| National Endowment for the Arts | |

Applications must be submitted in triplicate and mailed with other required materials to the address indicated under "Application procedures" for your category.

Category under which support is requested:
COLLABORATIVE PROJECTS

| Name (last, first, middle initial) | U.S. Citizenship |
| Brown, Joseph | Yes X   No   Visa Number |

Present mailing address/phone	Professional field or discipline
123 Main Street	Artist, Preparator
New York, NY 12345	(see background)
(212) 555-1111	**Birth Date** Place of Birth
	1-1-53 Raleigh, N.C.

Permanent mailing address/phone	Period of support requested
123 Main Street	Starting October 1, 1991
New York, NY 12345	month day year
(212) 555-1111	Ending October 1, 1992
	month day year

Career summary or background

Matthew Smith and Joseph Brown met while undergraduates at New York University in 1972. Their past collaborations include "REAPER-CUSSION," a musical performance for the Todd Ensemble at the Picasso Art Gallery in Rochester, New York, in June 1990, and, most recently, "Hyper-Space," a performance and installation at the Rosen-Fox Gallery in Buffalo, New York, in September 1990.

Matthew Smith is currently teaching drawing and painting at the State University of New York at Buffalo and is preparing for the "Albright-Knox Invitational" this March. Please see attached résumé.

Joseph Brown is working as a full-time artist and is a preparator at the West Museum in New York City. Please see attached résumé.

Amount requested from National Endowment for the Arts $5,000.00

Education			
Name of institution	Major area of study	Inclusive dates	Degree
New York University	drawing/printmaking	1972-1976	BFA
Yale University	drawing/sculpture	1976-1978	MFA

Fellowships or grants previously awarded

Name of award	Area of study	Inclusive dates	Amount

Present employment

Employer	Position / Occupation	Total income last calendar year
West Museum	Preparator, installationist	$7,200.00

Prizes / Honors received	Membership professional societies
Permanent collection—Missouri Art Center, 1977 Mural—Trade Center Observation Deck, 1979	

Description of proposed activity

(Do not complete this section if you are applying for an Artists', Craftmen's, or Photographers' Fellowship)

The goal of our collaboration is to produce a lively and harmonious relationship between the organic and inorganic aspects of our natural world.

Matthew Smith has created a series of drawings and musical pieces that express the atomic stucture of four elements taken from the Periodic Table of Elements (which is a mathematical inventory of the natural elements). The series is enhanced by the clean technical feel of the drawings and the "architectural" feel of the music, achieved by using Moog synthesizer and an electric piano in the building and reduction of tones.

Conversely, Joseph Brown's work projects the earthy textural resonance of animals as they interact among themselves.

The collaboration will involve the building of a scale environment (details are attached to the slide sheet). Through music, abstract depictions of animals will "interact" in the environment. The music will blend electronically synthesized sound with live recordings of animals, previously recorded on site in the Peruvian jungles. The drawings will be developed using the same methods as Matthew Smith's earlier works (using the Periodic Tables), by systematically scoring the pieces using the animals' spatial placement. The result will be a euphonious conversation between the living and nonliving world.

The interdisciplinary focus of the proposed installation will be amplified through the use of drawings, sculpture, and sound. The result will be a completely enveloping and engrossing environment.

Certification: I certify that the foregoing statements are true and complete to the best of my knowledge.

Signature of applicant _Joseph Brown_ Date _7/12/90_

Bibliography

Annual Register of Grant Support: A Directory of Funding Sources, 23rd Edition, 1990. Wilmette, IL: National Register Publishing Co., Macmillan Directory Division, 1989.

Bowser, Kathryn. *AIVF Guide to International Film and Video Festivals.* New York: Foundation for Independent Video and Film, 1988.

Grants and Awards Available to American Writers, 14th Edition. New York: PEN American Center, 1987.

Grants for Film, Media, and Communications. New York: Foundation Center, 1988.

Green, Laura R., Editor. *Money for Artists: A Guide to Grants and Awards for Individual Artists.* New York: ACA Books, 1987.

Lesko, Matthew. *Getting Yours: The Complete Guide to Government Money,* 3rd Edition. New York: Penguin Books, 1987.

Lyon, Richard Sean. *The Complete Book of Film Awards.* Los Angeles: Lyon Heart, 1990.

Money to Work: Grants for Visual Artists. Washington, DC: Art Resources International, 1988.

Index

Creative Writing: Poetry

Creative Writing: Translation

Dance

Design

Media Arts: Film

Media Arts: Video

Media Arts: Other

Multiple Arts Disciplines

Music: Composition

Music: Performance—Instrumental

Music: Performance—Vocal

Theater: Performance Art

Theater: Playwriting

Theater: Other